A Shared S

A SHARED SEARCH

Doing Theology in Conversation
with One's Friends

Maurice Wiles

SCM PRESS LTD

0 334 02559 1

First published 1994 by
SCM Press Ltd
26–30 Tottenham Road, London N1 4BZ

Typeset at The Spartan Press Ltd,
Lymington, Hants
and printed in Finland by
Werner Söderström Oy

Contents

Contents

Acknowledgments

The papers collected here first appeared as follows. I am grateful to the original publishers for permission to reproduce them.

1. For Christopher Evans: 'The Uses of "Holy Scripture"' in Morna Hooker and Colin Hickling (eds), *What about the New Testament?*, SCM Press 1975.

2. For Hans Frei: 'Scriptural Authority and Theological Construction: The Limitation of Narrative Interpretation' in Garrett Green (ed), *Scriptural Authority and Narrative Interpretation*, Fortress Press 1987. © 1987 Fortress Press. Used by permission of Augsburg Fortress.

3. For James Barr: 'Newton and the Bible' in John Barton and Samuel E. Balentine (eds), *Language, Theology and the Bible*, OUP 1994.

4. For William Frend: 'Orthodoxy and Heresy' in I. Hazlett (ed), *Early Christianity*, SPCK 1991.

5. For George Caird: 'Person or Personification? A Patristic Debate about Logos' in L. Hurst and N. Wright (eds), *The Glory of Christ in the New Testament*, OUP 1987.

6. For Henry Chadwick: 'Eunomius: "Hair-splitting Dialectician or Defender of the Accessibility of Salvation?"' in Rowan Williams (ed), *The Making of Orthodoxy*, CUP 1989.

7. For Gerard Rothuizen: 'On Being a Theologian in Today's Church' in *Het Leven is Meer dan Ethik*, J. H. Kok, Kampen 1987.

8. For Basil Mitchell: 'The Reasonableness of Christianity' in W. Abraham and S. Holtzer (eds), *The Rationality of Religious Belief*, OUP 1987.

9. For Peter Baelz: 'Worship and Theology' in D. W. Hardy and P. H. Sedgwick (eds), *The Weight of Glory*, T. & T. Clark 1991.

10. For Gordon Kaufman: 'Can Theology Still be About God' in S. Daveney (ed), *Theology at the End of Modernity*, Trinity Press International 1991.

11. For Schubert Ogden: 'In What Context Does it Make Sense to Say, "God Acts in History"?' in P. E. Devenish and G. L. Goodwin (eds), *Witness and Existence*, University of Chicago Press 1989. © 1989 by the University of Chicago. All rights reserved.

12. For Leander E. Keck: 'Can We Still Do Christology?' in A. Malherbe and W. Meeks (eds), *The Future of Christology*, Augsburg Fortress 1993. © 1993 Augsburg Fortress. Used by permission.

13. For John Hick: 'The Meaning of Christ' in Arvind Sharma (ed), *God, Truth and Reality*, Macmillan 1993.

Introduction

An invitation to contribute to a *Festschrift* is always likely to elicit a response of pleasure, even if the overall reaction it produces is sometimes of a more ambivalent character. For few things are more pleasing than to be asked to join in honouring a good friend and respected colleague. Yet the invitation may also be felt to be a distraction from some more long-term and substantial scholarly endeavour. And the university world today provides more than enough of such distractions already.

In the case of someone concerned with theology not only as a historical study but also as a contemporary discipline, some form of 'systematic theology' might well be assumed to be the kind of major work at which he or she should be aiming. A well-developed and fully argued account of Christian faith as it can reasonably and responsibly be given expression today would seem to be the most appropriate objective towards which such a theologian's studies should be directed. The disinclination of English scholars to produce works of that genre is often ascribed to an easy-going pragmatism, a lack of concern for the highest level of intellectual rigour.

But the writing of systematic theologies ought not to be thought of as necessarily the most appropriate, let alone the only proper goal of sustained theological endeavour. It is not a genre that was endemic to the patristic age. There was a time when Origen's *De Principiis* was described as the first work of Christian systematic theology, but more recent scholarship has firmly rejected any such description. It is better seen as an eclectic and experimental work, using the best available knowledge of the day to test out possible answers to a series of particular problems in the understanding of the relation of God to the world. The two

contexts in which the genre of systematic theology has flourished
most strongly have been mediaeval Christendom and post-
reformation protestantism. The mediaeval *Summae* themselves
had a more exploratory tone than some later readings of them
have allowed. But in any event they flourished on the basis of a
broadly agreed philosophical and religious outlook in the world
around them. Our own context could hardly be more different;
our world is philosophically and religiously fragmented.

It is with the protestant theologians of the seventeenth and
eighteenth centuries that the actual term, 'systematic theology',
first appears.[1] They could not build on as broad a consensus as
their mediaeval predecessors; but they could and did build on a
well-defined common basis of thought within their own church
communities. But even that context is hardly ours today. Church
communities are less homogeneous than they were, both religiously and theologically. Even within a particular confession or
denomination there is insufficient common ground to provide the
basis for a well-structured theological system. Scripture and
tradition may continue to provide the building-blocks of theological construction, but they are made of a more malleable material
than they used to be. The last two hundred years have seen too
many questions raised about the past, and about the ways in
which ancient texts can be read and assimilated into our present.
Scripture and tradition speak to us not with an authoritative,
disembodied voice as from heaven, but come to us in confused
and insidious ways through the prism of the corporate experience
of our community and the individual experience of each one of
us. The inevitably partial and subjective aspects of our theological knowing have to be acknowledged, but not simply
acquiesced in. The construction of a theological system rightly
seeks to overcome them, but it risks doing so in too premature
and too roughshod a manner; it tends simply to override them.
The manifold and deep-seated nature of the contemporary
challenges to the theological enterprise has to be explored more
sensitively than such a way of proceeding gives scope for. But for
anyone who believes in the unity of knowledge – and that means
for any monotheist – the abandonment of the possibility of a
systematic theology is not easily accepted. It may be unattainable

for us now, but it remains at least a theoretical goal. We may not be able to fit together all that we feel bound to say about God and the world into a coherent whole, but the attempt to do so remains an imperative that cannot simply be set on one side. We need to seek for a *via media* between the will o' the wisp of a publicly agreed and demonstrated orthodoxy on the one hand and the purely private creations of our own imaginings on the other. Theological construction always embodies a personal vision, even when that aspect of it is largely concealed by the formalized nature of its presentation. That is not something to be repented of, but it is something to be held in check. The test of difference between the properly personal and the private or cranky account is the degree to which we are prepared to attend to and to learn from the insights of others. The correction of the pejoratively subjective comes not by way of seeking some bogus ideal of pure objectivity, but along the road of inter-subjectivity. The fundamental character of theological knowledge means that it, perhaps more than any other form of human knowing, needs to be pursued as a cooperative venture, in which mutual respect and learning are the essential conditions of progress.

In the light of these reflections, it is not unreasonable to suggest that, so far from being a distraction from the serious work of systematic theology, the genre of *Festschrift* writing may be a particularly appropriate form of theological construction. We learn most from friends with whom we do not quite agree. Where our natural reaction to the critic or the polemicist is a defensive insistence on the already articulated views that are being challenged, we are more ready to entertain the idea that there may be something for us to learn by way of correction or modification from the friend who disagrees with us. We are predisposed towards that attitude which I have argued is essential for progress in theology. It has therefore seemed worthwhile to bring together here the papers that I have written for friends and colleagues in recent years, in the hope that together they may constitute a small contribution to theological construction. In almost every case the papers were written explicitly for the *Festschrift* in question and find their point of origin, in some cases substantially and in others secondarily, in the work of the person for whom they were written, and in discussions between us in the past. Their common theme is a search for an appropriate method for the work of constructive theology. Between them they touch on a number of central issues in theology, even if only in terms of how that issue can be appropriately tackled. Of course their coverage of theological topics, both in range and in depth, is very incomplete. Each was written as a quite separate paper for a particular occasion with no idea of their ever being brought together in this way. In this introductory essay I will try to stand back a little from them and ask how far, between them, they constitute a viable framework within which the work of theology might fruitfully be pursued today.

I have classified the papers under four headings, starting with the three familiar sources of Anglican theology – scripture, tradition and reason. But the way in which the three are understood to function and the balance between them are not as traditional as the classification. This follows from the changed role that scripture and tradition have to play in a contemporary theology. Those who in the past insisted on a place for reason as a third strand in the threefold cord were acknowledging the need for a right interpretation of scripture and tradition if they were to inform theology appropriately. Those first two sources could not fulfil their role without discrimination. But they were still seen as providing the raw material of revelation on the one hand and its guaranteed distillation on the other. The essential subject matter of theology was given there, even if not as straightforwardly given as some Christian expositors were wanting to claim. But it is that basic understanding of their role that has now to be called into question.

Christoper Evans was my New Testament colleague for only three short years. His work embodies an unusually rich blend of qualities: natural flair, a sharply critical acumen and a deep religious sensibility. The New Testament seen through his eyes became at the same time a more puzzling and a more religiously enlightening set of books; the one thing from which it seemed to be firmly disqualified was functioning as a repository of theological truth requiring only the interpreter's skill to bring it out into the open for proclamation as Christian truth to be believed. Other critical scholars have shown up the same sort of difficulty, for it is one that appertains to any attempt to continue to treat the New Testament as providing all that is needed for the determination of Christian doctrine. What was for me distinctive about Christopher Evans' handling of the New Testament was the way in which he showed how a negative evaluation of the New Testament as a repository of theological truth could go hand in hand with a deepening of its religious availability. The theologian might not be able to avoid having to learn to give a less determinative role to scripture in his theological work; but that process did not automatically involve a downgrading of its religious significance. In its embodiment of ancient wisdom and experience, and its provision of a focus of common sensibility for the church, and in many other such ways, it would still have a crucial role to play.

This questioning of the New Testament's role as a direct source of theological truth poses serious problems for the Christian theologian. The critical evaluation of the documents which has given rise to those problems is inescapable. But it is not surprising that some scholars, while fully accepting those critical findings, should have asked whether they need carry such stark theological consequences. One of the most sensitive and serious attempts to avoid those consequences has relied on the concept of narrative interpretation. The narrative character of much of the Bible is self-evident, and has always been an important element in its theological significance. Hans Frei was a seminal figure at the centre of a web of friends and former pupils who have developed various forms of that general approach. Being a beneficiary of Hans Frei's outstanding gift for friendship ensured that I took such an approach more seriously than I might otherwise have done. One could not but treat with great respect the suggestions of a man of such sensitivity both as a thinker and as a friend. The second paper was written for him as a paper of respectful dissent from that line of thought. For similar reasons the work of his close colleague, George Lindbeck, finds mention from time to time in these papers, because his approach represents the offer of an attractive way out of the theologian's apparent impasse, but one which I have felt bound to refuse; and I have tried to give my reasons for so doing. Scripture, as I have argued in the paper for Hans Frei, continues to be an important resource for the theologian, but there is no way back to older styles of reading – or way through to a second naïveté – which can reestablish it as the determinative source of what the theologian has to say. Its approaches are too variegated, and its diverse accounts of God and his dealings with us too integrally interwoven with no longer credible understandings of the world for it ever again to play its old role in a responsible theology. It cannot bear the weight that theologians in the past have placed upon it.

One of those who has most helped me over the years through personal conversation as well as through his published works to develop the kind of approach to biblical authority that finds expression in the paper for Hans Frei is James Barr, as the paper itself acknowledges. The paper I contributed to James Barr's *Festschrift* deals with a writer and a period that have played no part in the general run of my theological teaching and research. But Newton is a figure of intrinsic interest, and his approach to the Bible, which was of paramount importance to him and based on extensive study, is an illuminating example of how fundamentally any reading of the Bible, however honest and acute the reader, is affected by the assumptions and expectations of his or her own day. It is, I hope, an interesting historical vignette, but one with a theological sting in its tail. It is a story with a moral, which we are inclined to think we have now learnt, but which, I suggest, we may not have learnt as fully as we think we have. So the ending of the paper points forward to a question taken up more fully in the paper for Lee Keck in the theological section.

If scripture is multiform in character, the tradition of the church is still more so. Ecumenism has made it impossible to evade the problem by simply regarding one's own confessional tradition as the only one that need be taken seriously as embodying true Christian tradition. Indeed I have already argued that the diversity to be found within each confessional body is now so great, that even if such an attitude were possible it would not get over the difficulty with which the Christian theologian is faced. But there is one aspect of tradition to which appeal is still made in the search for a well-articulated Christian theology. The early councils antedate the divisions of the church into Catholic, Orthodox and Protestant; and the ecumenical creeds deriving from those councils have stood the test of time as accepted embodiments of Christian truth. The creeds have remained the touchstone of belief for the great majority of Christian confessions even in their isolation and mutual antagonisms, and are now playing an important role in furthering new trust and closer rapprochement between the churches. In them, it seems reasonable to claim, we have a guide through the maze of scriptural diversity that takes us to its common heart and provides a continuing framework for a systematic exposition of theology.

The period of early Christian thought to which the ecumenical creeds belong has provided the setting for most of my own more detailed historical studies. Seen through the eyes of historical research the creeds appear in a very different light. The three papers given here under the heading of tradition are offshoots of those historical studies. Though differing in genre from one another, each of them illustrates in a different way the kind of change in evaluation of the emergent Christian orthodoxy to which such study is likely to give rise. William Frend has been an unusually lively teacher of early church history, always insisting that those whose primary interest is in the development of Christian doctrine must see the story of that process in the context of the historical and social issues of the time. The paper written for him is a broad overview of early attitudes to heresy. What is clear even from a very general survey of that kind is the variety characteristic of early Christian belief. The old view that essential Christian doctrine was unchanging from the time of the apostles, with the creeds simply reaffirming that original doctrine against the malicious deviations of the heretics, does not begin to correspond with the historical evidence. There never was such an agreed pattern of apostolic belief.

George Caird took the place of Christopher Evans as a close New Testament colleague when I moved from London to Oxford. More conservative in his critical conclusions, he showed the same meticulous thoroughness in interpreting the New Testament text, whether his conclusions fitted comfortably with later orthodoxy or not – as the recollection with which the paper begins well illustrates. The paper itself shows two outstanding, and bitterly antagonistic, fourth-century writers arguing for the truth of their diametrically opposed theological positions from the text of the New Testament. Each of them can make out a plausible case for his own view, neither case proving decisive against the other – as theologians in conflict with one another have continued to do ever since. It is an illustrative example of a general truth. The proponents of orthodox doctrine (though in my example neither Eusebius nor Marcellus was judged fully orthodox!) may have claimed to establish their case as the only true interpretation of scripture, but in many instances the heretics they were seeking to repudiate could make out an equally convincing case for their views by appeal to the same scriptural tribunal.

The third paper was for Henry Chadwick, doyen of British patristic scholars for many decades and an invaluable personal teacher and guide to me throughout that time. Appropriately it makes my general point more decisively and more directly than the other two. It is commonly claimed that, even if the emergent orthodoxy was not identical with original apostolic teaching and even if it was not the only possible reading of the scriptural evidence, its essential validity and crucial importance lie in the fact that it alone represents a genuinely religious and not merely a rationalistic understanding of Christian truth. Nowhere is that claim more vigorously made than in relation to Arius, whose condemnation at the Council of Nicaea gave birth to the Nicene Creed (or perhaps one should say resulted in its conception, since the Nicene Creed as we know it actually saw the light of day at the later Council of Constantinople after half a century's gestation). It was the narrowly philosophical concerns of Arius (and of the later neo-Arian, Eunomius) which led them, it is argued, to views of God and of Christ which could never have sustained a living or a lasting faith. My own studies have convinced me that that is not true of Arius, and the paper included here argues that it is not true of Eunomius either. That view is not yet the received wisdom, though the general case in relation to most of the outstanding heretics (including Arius) is now widely accepted among scholars. The heretics were no less religious, no less concerned with the preservation of a lively faith (just as they were no less faithful to scripture) than those who won the day against them and so established themselves as the orthodox in the eyes of all future generations. Seeing them in that historical light, can we still regard the creeds which enshrine the victory of the orthodox over the heretics as providing the unquestionable framework of Christian truth for the contemporary theologian? Certainly there is much to be learned from the dedicated struggles of the early church to make coherent sense of the faith by which it lived and by which it transformed the world. But the lessons would seem to lie in the struggle rather than in the outcome – an outcome in which political and ecclesiastical power played so large a part alongside the theological debate.

So just as scripture is bound now to serve us as a general resource rather than as a decisive authority, so too tradition – even in its most exact form as constituted by the ecumenical creeds – seems destined to fulfil a similar role. Not everyone, it is true, who sees the theological story in the general way that I have described it draws the same conclusion. Another colleague, too young in years, though not in theological learning or friendship, to have been as yet the recipient of a *Festschrift*, Rowan Williams, presents as sympathetic a picture of Arius in his book that bears that name as anyone wishing to see the slanders and misrepresentations of past centuries put to rights could wish. Yet he still sees the creed that arose from the condemnation of Arius as fulfilling a vital role for the future well-being of the church.[2] In his view it serves to secure a true continuity of the historic faith, despite – or rather because of – its greater readiness to be innovative in its use of theological language; it helps to ensure a catholic rather than an academic character to the church. But I am not convinced. From the standpoint of later piety, itself substantially formed by the essentially Athanasian theology enshrined in the Nicene Creed, the judgment is a not unnatural one. But there is enough evidence to suggest a nascent 'Arian' piety that never had the chance to develop as the 'Athanasian' did. The tradition, it seems to me, might have taken a different direction at that point than the one it did take, without committing religious suicide in doing so.

If the picture that I have painted is at all correct, scripture serves the theologian as raw material not as finished product, and tradition provides him or her with further evidence but not with a verdict. Everything is still to play for. But the rules by which the next stage of the game is to be played are far from clear. The next paper in my collection reflects on the difficulties that such a situation poses. Gerard Rothuizen, to whom it was offered, was a Dutch scholar with a very different background and very different scholarly specialisms from my own. A minister of the Gereformeerde Kerk, his great interests were in ethics, in the war poetry of the first world war and in Dietrich Bonhoeffer. Yet he recognized the same dilemma of the contemporary theologian that I have outlined, though its contours looked very different from the angle from which he viewed it. His frequent letters, inexorably typed and in exotic English, were always full of memorable phrases and unexpected insights. He did not abjure the apologetic questions, but was more concerned that they should not exclude the religious affirmations, even if those had to be made in a form closer to the paradoxical style of his beloved poetry. No one, he would say to me, could suggest that I had overlooked the former; but there was scope for more of the latter. 'Don't', he once said as he disappeared round the door at the end of a visit, 'be afraid to appear sometimes a little pious.' But how to act on his advice? Scripture and tradition provide no forms of piety ready-made for the theologian's use any more than they provide a ready-made structure of belief. The theologian must use reason. But what form of reasoning is appropriate to the task that faces us? Is there a use of reason that will both find a way through the intellectual difficulties with which the theologian is faced and also lead to a responsible form of the 'piety' for which Gerard Rothuizen asked?

The nature of reasoning within a strictly deductive system is relatively easy to describe; the further it moves away from the deductive model, the more difficult the task becomes. The next two papers represent two attempts to trace out the contours of a use of reason appropriate to the theological task. They are appropriately written for my former Oxford colleagues in the philosophy of religion and in moral theology, both of whom gave generously of their wisdom and of their friendship during our years in office together. In the paper for Basil Mitchell I have tried to chart a place for the appropriate use of reason somewhere on a linear spectrum between rationalistic and fideistic extremes. There is no doubt that Basil Mitchell and I both stand nearer to the rationalistic than to the fideistic end of the spectrum. There was sufficient common ground (as well as sufficient difference) between us to explore the contours of what that appropriate use of reason might amount to in a series of seminars over a number of years. In the personal appreciation with which his *Festschrift* begins, Basil Mitchell is entitled 'The Reasonable Man'. Always judicious and careful in argument, his approach (much taught by Newman's illative sense) was never restrictive or confining. His reason never cut corners, but it often found ways through places where its narrower namesake had erected imperious 'No Thoroughfare' signs. Discussion with him did not remove my perplexity about how to proceed as a theologian, as the tribute to him acknowledges, but it did encourage the conviction that there are ways through the problems that beset us. We may need to inch our way forward rather than march in triumph down a well-mapped route, but there is reason to affirm that the path is not blocked.

As a fellow canon-professor Peter Baelz was colleague not only in the tasks of academic theology but also in the religious duties of a cathedral. That fact provides the context for my second attempt to chart the contours of a theologically appropriate use of reason. The model used there is not of a modulated linear scale but of a swing between opposing poles. Poetry and logic, imagination and argumentation – in neither pair can the two poles be coalesced, but each has a vital contribution to make to the wholeness of human understanding. So too with worship and theological reflection. Each needs the other, and each must have a place in the reasoning processes of theology. Peter Baelz integrated the two as sensitively as anyone I have known; there was a religious dimension to his philosophical reflection and a critical edge to his preaching. In that strange genre of the Bampton lecture-sermons, for which he was particularly well suited, he spoke movingly on behalf of the 'half-believer'. But the quality of that 'half-belief' had far more religious authenticity than the strident over-beliefs so prominent in today's world. This second model suggests a less well-controlled use of reason than the first, but it can perhaps do more to avoid the risk that one aspect of the multiform theological task may come to dominate the whole to the detriment of a true balance and a balanced view of truth.

Reflections of that sort can only prepare the way for the actual work of theological construction. What that will really involve can only be discovered in the process of attempting the work itself. The two central themes of Christian theology are God and Christ; indeed one might even describe the task of theology as a whole as the elucidation of the meaning of those two terms. The four final papers approach these two basic themes in the tentative and critical, but fundamentally hopeful, spirit for which the preceding reflections on scripture, tradition and reason call.

The question whether there is a reality indicated by the word 'God' is strictly speaking a prolegomenon to theology rather than a part of theology itself. Yet it is not just a philosophical preliminary to be got out of the way and then forgotten. For the nature of the search indicated by that question has implications for the substantive affirmations to be made about God. How, if at all, we can know about God affects what kind of things we can say about God. So the question of whether there is a referent for the word 'God' has its place also within theology itself, and the first of the four papers poses that question in its most fundamental form. My first knowledge of the work of Gordon Kaufman, for whom the paper was written, came through his appropriately entitled book, *The Problem of God*. And, as many of the scriptural writings bear witness, God is problematic for the person of faith and the theologian, as well as for the philosopher. Gordon Kaufman's subsequent writings have brought out very powerfully the role of imaginative construction in the theological task – particularly in its understanding of God. He has done this in so radical a manner that it is not always easy to be sure whether in the end the human construction constitutes an imaginative road of discovery or whether it is no more than a form of purely imaginative fantasizing. The paper argues for the former, which is indeed what Gordon Kaufman himself intends, though he would want to see it carried through in less straightforwardly personalistic terms than I have used here. I have attempted to make out my case with the aid of that broader style of reasoning, which the papers of the preceding section were trying to define. It is significant that the three theologians on whose thought it draws are all people grounded in a less analytic style of philosophical reflection (Neo-Thomist, Hegelian, and Hartshornian) than that in which I (and so many others in Britain) were reared. If these reflections do help to underwrite the validity of the theologian's work, they also carry with them a warning about how much of human (including Christian) reflection about God is over-ambitious or simply mistaken human imagining. Reassurance about the reality of the traditional goal of theology is accompanied by a reminder of how critical our theological appropriation of scripture and tradition needs to be.

The nature of the God to which such reflection points is not easily defined. Its grounding in the distinctive but not self-explanatory nature of our personal existence points to an ultimate mystery, not less than personal in character, in which being and goodness co-exist. The creative source of all that is is characterized by love. There is plenty of *prima facie* evidence against such a conviction, a good deal of which survives the '*prima facies*' or first look, and raises doubts once more about the reality of what is being affirmed. But there is no way by which those doubts can be definitively answered – either way. For the indirect and imaginative route by which all religious affirmations have come into being is a reminder that the language in which they find expression must be understood in equally indirect and imaginative ways. In the earlier paper for Basil Mitchell, I challenge Tony Kenny's sensitive and judicious exploration of the compatibility of omniscience and omnipotence, on the ground that the toughness of its reasoning is dependent on taking those terms in their literal sense. But the problem is not one of determining whether already fully understood senses of absolute sovereignty and perfect love are compatible; it is rather a question of whether our reflective religious intimations can suggest senses of such sovereignty and love in which the apparent areas of conflict are mitigated or even overcome.

For the Christian theologian the natural approach to that question is by way of reflection on what we know of God through the person of Christ. The fact points to another danger that besets the systematic theologian. The systematizer tends to think in a linear fashion. The system either begins with general reflections about God, and only when the true substance of those has been established moves on to affirmations about Christ; or it begins with Christ, as if no other source was relevant to the determination of our knowledge of God. But neither route can be followed with the undeviating directness of the Roman roadbuilder. Each approach needs the other. And in practice neither can, in a culture so deeply imbued with Christian culture as ours, be pursued without the other. If we think that we are doing so, we deceive ourselves.

So the papers in this section could have been ordered in other ways. But it is perhaps appropriate that the paper for Gordon Kaufman should be followed by one for Schubert Ogden, for they are the two writers who (though very different from one another) have most helped me develop my ideas about God's action, and have done so not only by their writings but also by close friendships which have always been accompanied by stimulating theological discussion among their other delights. God's action, in the forms of creation and providence, redemption and grace, lies at the very heart of scripture and tradition. Moreover the way in which a reasoned grounding of our affirmations about God draws on the most deeply personal aspects of our human existence seems to reinforce the appropriateness of a personalized concept of God such as lies at the heart of Christian faith. Yet the notion of God as personal agent is highly problematic. It seems impossible to affirm it today in the same specific manner that characterizes scripture and most of the tradition. Where such affirmation is attempted, it undermines the credibility of theological claims and gives to theology an air of unreality, a sense of failure to engage with the world as we find it to be. But where it is simply excised, that seems to undercut the religious nerve of what is being said; it leads to a different form of failure to engage with the world as we know it, but one just as corrosive of the theologian's intentions.

The paper for Schubert Ogden was an offshoot of a more extended discussion of the issue, which found publication in a book, *God's Action in the World* (SCM Press 1986), that I was writing at the same time. The approach suggested by the paper is that the problem cannot be satisfactorily dealt with as a single, comprehensive issue. It makes use of the distinction between the more poetic style of religious writing and the more analytic character of theological discourse, a distinction outlined in the earlier paper for Peter Baelz. The language functions differently in different contexts. And in none of them is it to be understood as if it were human action writ large. It is a form of speech designed to bring the strange concatenation of happenings in our universe and the wildly varied forms of human action into relation to that sovereign love from which they all ultimately derive and which continually sustains them in existence. How it is to be understood in relation to such a range of differing types of occurrence – quite apart from the problem of the varied genres of writing in which the notion may appear – is a matter for continuing sensitive discrimination.

The theme of divine action is one with which any systematic theology has to come to terms, because it is an aspect of every issue with which a systematic theology has to deal. Yet if my approach to it is right, it is a theme that will prove stubbornly resistant to systematization. Within such a genre as systematic theology it is likely to be pressed into unduly uniform usage and even more likely to be heard in inappropriate ways. The nature of the problems it poses invites a range of exploratory discussions in the spirit of Origen's *De Principiis* rather than the formal treatment of a *Summa* or a systematic theology.

If the figure of Christ is integral to Christian reflection on the co-existence of sovereignty and love, it is even more integral to Christian reflection on the concept of God's action. No wonder that christology stands at the centre of most systematic theologies. I have already suggested that reflection on the twin themes of God and of Christ could be said to constitute the whole subject-matter of theology, and christology in its narrower sense is precisely concerned with the relation of the two to one another. But much discussion of the topic is highly unsatisfying; standard accounts often do more to clarify the heretical views which must not be maintained than to bring to life what should be said. It seems as if there must be something wrong about the way the issue is traditionally posed for theological discussion. The paper for Lee Keck raises that question in its most fundamental form, much as the paper for Gordon Kaufman does in relation to God; but it comes up with a more disconcerting answer.

Lee Keck was my host for an enjoyable stay at Yale Divinity School, but being a New Testament scholar (and never a colleague as Christopher Evans and George Caird were) he has had less influence on my thinking than any other of those for whom the papers in this collection were written. A remark of his may have been the occasion that triggered off the paper, but as a whole it does not bear the stamp of his influence. The problem the paper tackles is not a new one, but it is one that has certainly not lost its force. 'Christ' is a term with a rich variety of connotations. It refers to Jesus; but it refers also to a cosmic reality, the source and inner sustaining power of the created order, and to a mystical reality, embodied in the church and encountered in the experience of prayer. But do we have the resources to affirm and speak of a single reality of this multi-dimensional kind? Do scripture and tradition, as we are now coming to understand them, point to a single Christ, to whom all the varied forms of christological affirmation can be applied? May it not be that just as the varied forms of divine action, of which the tradition speaks, need to be understood not uniformly but in a carefully modulated variety of ways, so too the various types of affirmation about Christ need to be understood not in relation to a single specifiable reality, whose 'person' is, albeit imperfectly, defined in christology, but rather as ways of indicating that the same sovereign love of God that has been so transformatively apprehended in the figure of Jesus is the unifying power present in all those varied forms of divine action?

John Hick is a friend who both by his writings and by personal discussion has always challenged me to consider whether the context of my theological reflection may not be too narrowly circumscribed. He has rightly insisted over many years that such reflection needs to take the teachings and practices of other religions into its purview, and has raised for me, as for many others, the question of what the implications of those other religions are for the traditional Christian affirmations about Christ. How are those other religions to be related both to God and to Christ? The ensuing public discussion of that issue, which John Hick's work has done so much to stimulate, illustrates clearly the confusion to which the multivalent designation 'Christ' can give rise. In the paper offered to him I have tried to tease out the nature of that confusion. It provides just one illustration of the difficulties that arise from failing to recognize the varied uses which the term 'Christ' can serve in differing contexts.

Those four papers do not take us very far along the path of constructive theology. If the first three sections represent a selection and honing of the appropriate tools for the job, the last section represents a levelling of the ground and clearing away of obstructions. The actual work of building remains to be done. The systematic theologian is like a Solomon embarking on the building of a temple. But the temple played a somewhat ambiguous role in Israel's history. Perhaps our God does not dwell in a temple built with human hands or with human words. The alternative approach, characteristic of Origen's *De Principiis*, suggests rather the building of temporary tents, to be used for a short time but soon to be taken down as we move on into the next stage of our wilderness journey. It is an approach that, as Origen discovered, has never been popular in the church and is not likely to prove so now. But it is not clear that it ought to be so unwelcome. In its earliest days Christianity was spoken of as 'The Way' and the image of a journey has always played an important role in spiritual writings. We neither can nor are intended to sit at ease in Zion. So it is not unfitting that the work of theology should share this general characteristic of a journeying faith.

But it would be a mistake to speak as if the constructive

theologian were setting out to produce a brand new building from scratch, of whatever degree of solidity or permanence. The rich resources of scripture and tradition provide much of its potential structure and many of its building blocks, even if there is need for a good deal of modification and reconstruction, and not a little demolition. So even the removal of obstructions is not just preparation for the work of building; it is a genuine part of constructive theology itself. Thus if the papers for Schubert Ogden and for John Hick do succeed in dealing with the difficulties they raise, they do not leave us with nothing, with a *tabula rasa*. They may better be seen as releasing the religious concept of vocation for more intelligible and constructive use in the direction of human lives, and as opening the way for a more positive attitude to other faiths, an attitude that has always been present, though in concealed and muted fashion, within Christianity's monotheistic faith and its affirmations about the universal role of the divine Logos.

So it may be that theology is best done in this more tentative exploratory manner, in which the theologian tries to find a way through some of the difficulties for understanding and for practice that are encountered in the accepted forms of faith. One of the criteria that the vital appeal to reason imposes is the criterion of consistency, both between the various theological explorations of this kind, and between them as a whole and other areas of human knowledge. It is that necessity that fuels a drive in the direction of a more systematic theology. But if that is its motivation, then the kind of construction to which it points needs to be seen not so much as providing houses for the church to dwell in, but rather as testing the consistency, and thereby the validity, of more particular theological reflections. Its proper role is to serve theological enquiry, not to crown it by replacing it. Exploratory enquiry (itself serving the way of faith) is nearer to the heart of the matter. And that, as I have argued earlier, needs to be pursued not just in the isolation of the theologian's own private reflections but in active conversation with others. It is in the hope that they may serve as an exemplar of that kind of approach to theology (however their particular contents may be assessed) that these *Festschrift* papers have been brought together for publication.

Part One

Scripture

I

The Uses Of 'Holy Scripture'

Is *'Holy Scripture' Christian*? is certainly a striking title for a theological book.[1] Christopher Evans himself describes it apologetically as a 'perhaps foolish title'.[2] It has a recognizably impish quality about it, but characteristically it poses a question that is searching, even uncomfortable, but far from foolish.

In the course of Christian history the distinctive character of 'holy scripture' has often been asserted in ways which were epistemologically absurd and religiously disastrous. Its composition has been ascribed to forms of dictation which left the human writer no more than an instrument in the hand of the divine author but ensured the inerrancy of the resultant text. Then in obedience to its commands witches have been burnt to the glory of God or else a divine authority claimed for all one's own immediate concerns by the Midas touch of allegorical interpretation. Modern scholarship has learnt long since to eschew all such excesses. But the distinctive character of 'holy scripture' is still frequently linked to accounts of revelation that carry less than universal assent. Christopher Evans gives one such example in his discussion of Cullmann's book *Salvation in History*.[3] Professor Mitchell has recently suggested that if the concept of divine inspiration of the Bible is to be retained, it will need to take the form of a belief 'that there are truths which men could not have discovered by themselves, but which God has found means of communicating to them'.[4] I do not intend to discuss here whether any account of inspiration or revelation of this kind can be sustained which would justify something like the degree of distinctiveness traditionally ascribed to 'holy scripture'. That task is one that appears to me to be a good deal more difficult than it is often assumed to be.

But in this paper I want to pursue a different question. It is this: suppose one were unable to provide any such account, would it follow that one ought to abandon the idea of a canonical scripture altogether? Or would there still be a place for a 'holy book' in the practice of Christian faith? Other religions which have very different ideas of revelation from the Christian tend to have their 'holy books' too. While the particular role of the Christian scriptures is undoubtedly related to the particular Christian understanding of revelation and of the unique incarnation of God in Jesus Christ, it would be surprising if Christianity's holy book did not function within Christianity in ways comparable with the role of holy books in other religious traditions. I propose therefore to offer some rather broad reflections on the way in which a holy book is liable to function in a religious culture, to consider how far the Bible functions in that kind of way and finally to attempt some evaluation of it in relation to those functions. I shall set out my reflections under three headings.

1. *Respect for antiquity*

Change always involves an element of loss. Even where change is clearly desirable, the past was seldom wholly evil and past good is often lost (it may be inevitably) along with the excision of the evil. Enthusiastic supporters of the New English Bible will normally be prepared to admit that where it replaces the Authorized Version there is loss as well as gain. In a pre-literate society where change is slow and the greatest danger is loss of old skills, religion is likely to fulfil an important conservative role. The myths speak of a golden age in the past, and much religious practice is designed to preserve or recapture it. Writing is an enormously important tool for this kind of preservative function. Books, when they first began to appear, would have had, in addition to their practical value, an aura of rarity and mystery which they cannot possibly have for us in an age of the paperback and the popular press. I remember a Nigerian student at the University of Ibadan, himself a first generation literate, telling me of the sense of shock with which in his first weeks at the University he had heard one of his tutors say that he did not agree with what a published book said. His sense of shock was very similar to that which a fundamentalist Christian might feel on hearing for the first time someone say that he thought the Bible was wrong in some particular respect.

The charge of novelty is a powerful weapon in making a religion look ridiculous. Celsus used it against Christianity; Roman Catholics (in less ecumenical days) used to use it against Protestants; and main-line Protestants use it against Christian Scientists and Jehovah's Witnesses. The Old Testament scriptures were important to the infant Christian church not only for internal guidance, but as a way of providing external respectability, of showing that Christianity was a religion with a past. On the whole people don't write 'scripture'; they write (very possibly believing themselves to be doing so by inspiration of the Spirit), but time has to pass before what they have written becomes 'scripture'. If they want to write scripture they do so pseudepigraphically in the name of some past saint or hero, or else they find it conveniently hidden in the temple.

Thus a written record hints at the changeless, primaeval character of religion; it suggests that religion is concerned with the eternal rather than the ephemeral. It is a standing corrective against the shallowness of a religion that in its passionate concern with the present moment has lost its hold on that dimension.

That is an important function; and a religion without holy scriptures would be in grave danger of losing something vital. But can they fulfil that role without at the same time doing even greater harm? New knowledge arises; moral standards change (often for the better). The immorality of Homer's gods, for example, came to be regarded as intolerable. His poems as a result were to be excluded from Plato's ideal republic and he himself consigned (as in Pythagoras' dream) to Hades, where he was depicted suspended from a tree and surrounded by serpents, together with those who had neglected their wives, because of the things he had said about the gods.[5] Alternatively his lively stories could be allegorized into cosmogonical myths as by the Stoics. Christians too have often become involved in similar spiritual contortions, and indeed still do so to this day as pious congregations find themselves exulting in the hope of vengeance upon Babylon and singing, 'Blessed shall be he that taketh thy children and throweth them against the stones.'[6]

But there are other, less obvious, dangers too. Plato's suspicion of books, that characterized his later years, was more broadly based than simply on his objection to the immorality of Homer's gods. Books could never fully express the doctrine they were intended to convey; some readers were sure to misunderstand them and the book was unable to defend or to explain itself.[7] Moreover once books come to be revered as authorities, they encourage false short-cuts to knowledge. A. D. Nock declared that 'throughout the imperial period one of the conspicuous features of intellectual life is a readiness to accept statements because they were in books or even because they were said to be in books'.[8] So in later centuries the writings of Aristotle were regarded as rendering otiose the careful observations of the naturalist. Once grant that your book has the authority of God himself and such tendencies will be further exaggerated. Economic research and moral enquiry are not of central importance if the holy book already contains for you the essential insights into the proper ordering of society and an unchanging code of ethical behaviour. The use of the Bible to strengthen the forces of reaction is written large on the pages of history.

Now there is of course much else within the pages of the Bible that not only permits but insists on radical change. The New Testament's critique of the Old carried within it an implicit protest against the very way in which it has itself so often been regarded in the past. That respect for the past which the very existence of a holy scripture embodies and makes effective must for the Christian be dialectically combined with the ruthless criticism of life lived in the Spirit, that wind whose source and destination no man can tell.

2. *Escape from subjectivity*

For the most part the religious believer has (or should have) a healthy distrust of his own subjective judgments. He seeks escape from the smallness and the sinfulness implicit in a purely private, personal perspective. His faith is in that which is other than and greater than himself. He longs for objectivity, a sense of his faith as something given rather than something self-induced. So he sees holy scripture not merely as something coming to him with the givenness that belongs to the past as a whole; it is in some special way given by God. Thus the Old Testament law was not only found in the temple, some of it at least was written with the finger of God. A part of the Egyptian *Book of the Dead* was similarly found under a statue of the god Thoth and written in the writing of the god himself.[9] The Qur'an too was dictated by the angel Gabriel; and, as if that were not sufficient, later tradition (in direct contradiction of the text of the Qur'an itself) went on to recount how Muhammad ascended into heaven and received it directly from the very hands of God.[10]

But however strong the insistence on a direct divine source of holy scripture, it has never long been possible to avoid a balancing emphasis on the need for divine illumination of the reader also. Thus the Calvinist tradition has emphasized the need for the '*testimonium internum spiritus sancti*' and we find a Muslim Sufi declaring that 'no understanding of the Holy Book is possible until it is actually revealed to the believer as it was revealed to the prophet'.[11]

Such developments force us to ask how effectively a written record can fulfil its role as a source of genuine objectivity. Men certainly can evade its force by allegorical or other means and often do so, albeit unconsciously. Nevertheless it is some sort of check. It takes some getting round. Words have a firmer shape of meaning than symbolic acts or visual representation. And this, I take it, is at least a part of what lies behind the insistence of the Reformed tradition on the primacy of audition over against vision as the model by which knowledge of God ought to be construed – a theme much emphasized by Professor Torrance in his recent writings.[12] Words, and still more written words, have a tougher element of objectivity about them. We may be able to escape their implications by self-deception, but we would deceive ourselves more easily without them.

In the *Confessions* of Augustine there is an instructive discussion which serves to show how limited this provision of

objectivity is. It is easier, he argues, to be confident of the fact of
God's creation of all things visible and invisible than it is to be
certain of what Moses intended by the opening verses of the book
of Genesis. Our primary concern therefore has to be with what is
true rather than with what is the meaning of the written text. He
goes on:

> When [a man] says 'Moses did not mean what *you* say, but
> what I say,' and then does not deny what either of us says but
> allows that *both* are true – then, O my God, life of the poor, in
> whose breast there is no contradiction, pour thy soothing balm
> into my heart that I may patiently bear with people who talk
> like this! It is not because they are godly men and have seen in
> the heart of thy servant what they say, but rather they are
> proud men and have not considered Moses' meaning, but only
> love their own – not because it is true but because it is their
> own.[13]

We are in no position to tell how fair Augustine is being to his
critics. But there is no denying the shrewdness of his psychological insight. Men do undoubtedly read back their own
meanings into the sacred text. And their capacity for doing so,
albeit in good faith and without, at least at the conscious level, the
perverted motives which Augustine ascribes to his opponents, is
no harmless eccentricity. For having once convinced themselves
that their meaning is the objective meaning of the sacred text,
they then hold it with a renewed fanaticism as something which
comes to them with the direct authority of God himself. It is a
high price to pay for something that originates in a proper desire
to escape from the dangers of subjectivity.

The question that then forces itself upon us is this. Can we be
free of such dangers while still holding on to 'holy scripture' as a
symbol of that objectivity, that otherness, that address to us
which is at the heart of faith in a personal God? If we should no
longer find it possible to see the Bible as characterized by that
distinctive form of divine address which theories of inspiration
have attempted to delineate, or if we have already become fully
aware of the way in which any such divine address is inextricably
intermingled with the fallibility of its human form both in its

original expression and in its interpretation, can the concept of 'holy scripture' still fulfil such a role even symbolically? Or would any such idea be more likely to mislead than to serve the cause of truth?

3. *Focus of community*

Homer may have been consigned by Pythagoras to Hades, but the primary school-children of the Hellenistic world were made to inscribe in their exercise books, as their first essay in writing, the words 'Homer was not a man but a god.'[14] The poetic tradition, with Homer at its heart, provided for the Hellenistic age 'a fundamental homogeneity which made communication and genuine communion easier'. Men had in common 'the same metaphors, images, words – the same language'.[15] It ensured a basic unity of culture, in much the same way that the Bible and Shakespeare did in England a hundred years ago.[16]

In the same sort of way a fixed canon (like a fixed liturgy) provides a focus of unity for the Christian community, a common source of religious imagery; it needs to be large enough to provide for the rich variety of men's religious needs but compact enough to function as a source of common sensibility.

Its importance as a unifying agent can be illustrated historically. The fixing of the Mosaic canon is linked with Ezra's rebuilding of the Jewish state in conscious opposition to the surrounding peoples. It is no coincidence that the final fixing of the Jewish canon follows so swiftly on the heels of the fall of Jerusalem. The creation of the Christian canon was connected with the need to deal with the threats posed by Marcionites and by Gnostics.

But that method of securing unity over against the challenge of heretical ideas has its limitations. It is a card you can play only once. Having made the canon large enough to rule out Marcion and selective enough to deal with the Gnostics, there was need to find some other way of responding to the later challenges of an Arius or a Luther.

But there are more subtle dangers than those associated with the problem of heresy. The literary canon that is compact enough to be the basis of a common culture is unlikely to be rich enough to sustain that role indefinitely. The kind of situation which may then arise is vividly depicted by Peter Brown in his description of the Roman writer in the age of Augustine:

> Such a man lived among fellow-connoisseurs who had been steeped too long in too few books. He no longer needed to be explicit; only hidden meanings, rare and difficult words and elaborate circumlocutions, could save his readers from boredom, from *fastidium*, from that loss of interest in the obvious, that afflicts the overcultured man . . . Above all, the narrow canon of acknowledged classics had been charged with a halo of 'Wisdom': an intellectual agility quite alien to modern man, would have to be deployed constantly to extract the inexhaustible treasure that, it was felt, must lie hidden in so cramped a quarry.[17]

The natural outcome for the Christian writer in Augustine's day was the regular use of fanciful interpretations of an allegorical kind. But in eschewing the vagaries of allegorical method, we have not thereby freed ourselves from the fundamental problem. Are not some of the difficulties faced by the Roman writer whom Peter Brown describes shared by the authors of the continuous stream of biblical commentaries today? Do not many New Testament interpreters find themselves more or less forced into putting forward far-fetched interpretations in the desperate hope of saying something new, of being 'original' in the sense demanded by examinations for the Doctorate of Philosophy? The way in which a fixed canon provides a shared resource of faith and spirituality for all Christians is a blessing, but it is a mixed blessing.

These are not, of course, the only functions that holy scripture might serve in Christian faith. I have not attempted to explore uses of scripture which arise primarily from the distinctiveness of Christianity. But they seem to me to be three significant ways in which holy books in general, and the Bible in particular, have functioned. All three are religiously important functions which ought to find a place within the life of the church, even though they also have their inherent dangers. If 'holy scripture' is given too absolute a position, then the good that it can convey is likely to be outweighed by the evil that it can also bring with it. But it does not need to be given an absolutist position for the fulfilment of these three roles.

If then these are proper ways of understanding the role of holy scripture within Christian faith, what implications do they have for the interpretation of scripture? The Bible, we are sometimes told, should be studied and interpreted as any other book. That demand is one way of expressing the insistence that the Bible must not be exempted in deference to false piety from all appropriate forms of critical enquiry. But it is not a very satisfactory way of making the point. For how does one interpret 'any other book'? We do not interpret all books indentically. To interpret a legal statute is not the same thing as to interpret a novel. They exist for different purposes and we therefore ask different questions of them in the two processes, although we use the one word 'interpretation' for them both.

What then would be involved in interpreting the Bible as 'holy scripture' in the light of the reflections that I have been pursuing here? It would mean discussing it and drawing out its meaning in ways which would enable it to function for us in the three ways that I have tried to describe. This would involve first of all letting it recall for us the primaeval nature of those religious traditions out of which our faith comes and for which God cares as fully as he cares for us and for the future. There would be no call to feel ashamed of or try to cover up elements that seem to us strange or crude because they belong to the comparatively primitive origins of religious belief. These would not be in conflict with its role as holy scripture; they would be a proper part of it.

Secondly it would involve letting the Bible symbolize for us the 'over-against-ness' of God. This role stands closest to the traditional understanding of its authority as conveying otherwise inaccessible and wholly reliable knowledge of God. How can such a role continue in a symbolic way once we have come to recognize the need to use our critical judgment and discrimination in determining what is true and what is applicable to our own situation in the biblical record? We would need to be able to see it as something which addresses us in ways that we could not have thought up or invented for ourselves. That is a characteristic of all great literature and of any worthwhile account of occasions of great significance from past history – and clearly on any account the Bible is both those things. It would involve in addition the conviction that the literature and the events recorded are of a kind which (whatever else they may have done) have given rise to true belief about and response to God and have the potentiality of continuing to do so.

Thirdly it would involve seeing the Bible as a common resource of life and spirituality, the provider of a unity of feeling among Christian people. To facilitate its use in this way, what would be called for would be an imaginative development and assimilation of its leading themes and images. This is something that could co-exist (as indeed to some extent it already does) with very great diversity of specific beliefs. No canon, as we have seen, can ever fulfil such a function perfectly. Any selection of writings as an agreed corpus for such a purpose is bound to be somewhat arbitrary. But nor is it something that can be artificially determined by decree from on high. Attempts of that kind to impose a canon are doomed to failure. It is something that has to grow. In the canon of scripture the Christian church has such a growth. Seen in this context the restriction of the canon might more readily be grasped as blessing and not the 'curse of the canon' that Christopher Evans himself has been heard on occasion to describe it.

Critical study of the Bible has often been felt to be in conflict with its role as 'holy scripture'. So, on certain understandings of what constitutes something 'holy scripture', it has often been. It does not cohere readily with the conception that a holy book is first and foremost an authoritative utterance of special divine origin. But in relation to the uses that I have outlined here it would more readily appear as a tool in the service of 'holy scripture'.

2

Scriptural Authority and Theological Construction: The Limitations of Narrative Interpretation

The question is not whether scripture has authority for Christians. That it has is an analytic truth. Inherent in the designation of certain writings as scripture is an affirmation of their authoritative status.[1] The question is what kind of authority can rightly be ascribed to them. For authority can take many forms, and more than a few of those forms cannot properly be attributed to the Christian scriptures.

If we are to throw any light on this well-worn problem, it will be useful to place the issue in a broad historical perspective. The motives that gave rise to the initial emergence of an authoritative Christian scripture were, no doubt, mixed. The story can be presented as a quenching of the Spirit, a way of protecting the church from the kind of disconcerting prophetic challenge with which Jesus himself had faced the Judaism of his day. With Christopher Evans we may feel an urge to speak of the 'curse of the canon'.[2] But that would be at most a very partial presentation of the story – if a useful corrective to some uncritical versions of it. For the emergence of the Christian scriptures was the outcome also of a laudable concern to ensure that the faith not be led astray by the siren voices of contemporary cults or theosophies but remain true to its roots in the person of Jesus and the initial teaching of the apostles. But once the scripture was established as an indispensable authority in relation to faith, the nature and extent of that authority did not cease to develop. All authorities have a tendency to overreach themselves. We know that to be widely true of people in authority; and since it is people who operate institutional forms of authority, it is true of them also. So there was a rapid expansion of the range of issues on which scripture was expected to speak. The history of early biblical exegesis shows scripture being asked to give precise answers to questions with which it was hopelessly ill-suited to deal. The result was an overexegesis, which, since the answers it was being expected to produce had to come from somewhere, inevitably took the form of eisegesis. So although scripture provided the *form* of authority, the *substance* came more and more from the ecclesiastical powers who determined the tradition of how scripture was to be understood. The Reformation sought to rescue scripture from this subservience to ecclesiastical authority, and did so primarily by an appeal to its literal sense. But however effective such a move may have been in its immediate objective challenging established ecclesiastical tradition, it had its own difficulties to contend with. It was not a very successful court of appeal in debate with Socinians or later Unitarians.[3] But the extent of its shortcomings came to light only more gradually, in the course of the attempt to come to terms with the rise of biblical criticism, described with masterly insight by Hans Frei in *The Eclipse of Biblical Narrative*.

It is not my purpose here, nor do I have the competence, to undertake detailed discussion of that complex story. But some very general points need to be made in the light of it as we approach the question of how we ought to understand the authority of scripture today. There has never been a golden age when scripture has functioned in an unproblematic manner in the life of the church. There have always been attendant difficulties. So if we find the issue beset with difficulty, we are not in that respect in a totally different position from our forebears in the faith. On the other hand, critical study of the Bible has enabled us to see things about the nature of the scriptural texts which were not so evident before and whose general truth cannot seriously be questioned. The new insights are of many kinds: the rootedness of the texts in the particular sociocultural understanding of their times; the variety of theological standpoints represented by the various scriptural authors; the differing degrees of historical accuracy characteristic of different scriptural writings. The shifts of understanding so baldly summarized here are extensive and cannot fail to affect the way in which the writings can function as authoritative scripture. We may not be in a *totally* different position from our forebears in the faith, but we are in a *significantly* different position. Neither theology nor the church more generally has yet taken the full measure of that significant difference. They have not come fully to terms with the new situation in which they find themselves. They still expect scripture to fulfil essentially the same role in the life of the church that it has fulfilled in the past, establishing the church's doctrine and providing firm guidance for its practical life. But the criticial stance accepted by the great majority of scholars does not fit easily with that expectation. Where such a critical approach is broadly accepted in the church, it would seem that scholarly authorities must now control the way scripture is to be understood, as the ecclesiastical authorities used to do, and those scholarly authorities are in important respects less well oriented to mediate scripture in a form that will serve the deeper needs of men and women. It is not surprising that there are calls for a new reformation to free the scriptures once again, this time from the papacy of the scholar.[4]

Biblical scholars do not want to keep the scriptures to themselves. It would hardly be in their professional interest to do so. And more important, most of them embarked upon their field of study because of the religious value they apprehended in scripture as it was functioning in the life of the church. Various strategies have been designed specifically to address the problem of how scripture, critically understood, can continue to serve the needs of the church. In that aim, movements often contrasted as 'radical' and 'conservative' can be seen to be at one. Thus it was the aim of both Bultmann's programme of demythologization and the 'biblical theology' movement to present the heart of the scriptural message in a form appropriate for contemporary belief and action. Each approach has serious limitations that have been rehearsed often enough to need no further repetition here. What is more significant for our purpose is the way in which the two approaches sought to deal with the problem posed by the critical

exegesis of the Bible, on the one hand, and the church's
expectation of an authoritative role to be fulfilled by scripture, on
the other. Certainly there was no repudiation of the critical
approach as such. But there was an attempt to find a form of it
that would enable the Bible to continue to fulfil something very
like its traditional role in the life of the church. Thus it was the
understanding of scripture rather than its role in the life of the
church that was the prime candidate for modification.

That way of approaching the task still dominates the theological scene. Today there are those who look to 'narrative
interpretation' to achieve the goal that has eluded earlier
attempts. Critical study of the Bible, it is rightly claimed, has been
conducted too exclusively in terms of *historical* criticism. Not all
the scriptural writings are historical in character, except in the
trivial sense that they all come from the past. But they are all
writings, varied forms of literature. Any insights from literary
criticism are therefore to be welcomed as likely to redress the
balance and correct the lopsidedness resulting from over-
emphasis on historical criticism. A more balanced approach,
it may be hoped, will have the potential to overcome the present
impasse, without requiring any repudiation of the valid insights
of earlier critical work.

Narrative interpretation is a particularly attractive form of
literary assessment for the biblical scholar, because it con-
centrates on a category of literature that stands close to historical
writing. In particular it is readily applicable to the Gospels,
which, if not 'history' in a strict sense (as we are constantly
reminded they are not), are certainly, in Frei's phrase, 'history-
like'.[5] There is no question about the value of such an approach
to certain scriptural writings that are of a clearly narrative form.
But narrative interpretation is being pressed into far wider service
at the present time. 'Narrative', says Ronald Thiemann, 'high-
lights both a predominant literary category within the Bible and
an appropriate theological category for interpreting the canon as
a whole'.[6] The wider role must indeed be claimed for narrative if
the approach is to make a significant contribution to our more
general problem. And that is certainly what Thiemann looks to it
to provide. 'The turn to narrative', he asserts a little later, 'is one

way of providing an alternative to that predominant modern tradition' which affirms 'the primacy of anthropology in modern theology'.[7] But can narrative properly fulfil this larger task?

Thiemann is by no means alone in looking to it to do so. Thus Charles Wood speaks of how the 'overall narrative character of the canon . . . suggests that the canon might plausibly be construed as a story which has God as its "author"'.[8] And George Lindbeck answers his own question. 'What is the literary genre of the Bible as a whole in its canonical unity?' by claiming that the diverse materials contained within it 'are all embraced, it would seem, in an overarching story that has the specific literary features of realistic narrative'; he then goes on to describe the 'primary function of the canonical narrative' as ' "to render a character . . . , offer an identity description of an agent" namely God'.[9] To treat scripture in this way is not something that can easily be done without going back on the genuine insights that critical study has engendered. All the authors I have cited are well aware of the difficulties involved but believe that they can in fact be overcome. In my view the difficulties are more damaging than the authors believe.

It needs to be said at the outset that there is no necessary unity to the contents of the canon apart from the fact that they are the documents to which the church has chosen to ascribe an authoritative status as scripture. The process of that choice was a gradual one lasting more than two centuries, with different concerns predominating at different times. It has certainly been claimed from early times that the scriptural writings do constitute a unity, but whether they really do is an entirely different matter. Wood is very conscious of this and speaks of the hermeneutical use of the canon as grounded in a 'decision' to 'read scripture *as if it were a whole*, and as if the author of the whole were God'.[10] On the face of it, the double 'as if' suggests a twofold arbitrariness. In the past when the divine authorship of scripture was affirmed without any qualifying 'as if', it could serve as a justification for reading scripture as a whole, however difficult the task itself might prove to be. Wood's use of the 'as if' may save him from having to produce an account of divine inspiration to give specific substance to the concept of divine authorship, but it also prevents him from using the claimed divine authority in an explanatory role in relation to the reading of scripture as if it were a whole. The quasi-divine authorship is a part of the description of what we decide to do, not a reason for the decision. As Thiemann points out, some attempt is made to rescue the act of decision from sheer arbitrariness by claiming that this way of reading scripture is to read it in its 'literal sense', where literal sense is understood as that 'sense whose discernment has become second nature to members of the community'.[11] But two problems assail such a claim. In the first place, it is questionable how close Wood's narrative reading of the canon under the influence of modern literary theory really is to the way it was read in precritical times.[12] But even setting that difficulty aside, the claim does not help very much towards getting rid of the arbitrariness of the decision. For it amounts simply to saying that it is a decision to go on regarding scripture as it has been regarded in the past, whatever new insights about its nature may have arisen in the meantime.

Having once made the decision that scripture is to be read as a unity, there is still a choice to be made about the nature of that unity. 'Narrative', as Thiemann puts it, 'is one of a number of possible images round which the diverse materials of the canon can be organized.'[13] The choice is not a straightforward one. There are many elements within the canon, such as the wisdom literature, which do not easily fall within such a category. Moreover, even within the more explicitly narrative material that certainly bulks large within the scriptural corpus, there is, as Thiemann rightly points out, the further problem of the 'irreducible diversity of the integral narratives' that are found there.[14] Nevertheless, if a choice of category has to be made, the choice of narrative is not unreasonable. Narratives or stories can be wide ranging and allow for various subplots within an ordered whole. But when the concept of narrative is applied as broadly as it is in its application to the canon as a whole, it is questionable whether it is right to claim of it at that level, as Lindbeck does, that it 'has the specific literary features of realistic narrative'. The term when applied to the whole of scripture has been stretched beyond the point at which such precise description is appropriate.

But more significant is the difficulty of determining how this varied literature is to be read as one story. Lindbeck speaks of the 'canonical narrative' as if, once the possibility of speaking in such terms has been raised, the substance of the story is clear. Almost any combination of things can be read as one story, given sufficient ingenuity – just as the later findings of science *could* be incorporated into a Ptolemaic understanding of the universe, given sufficient epicycles, special cases, etc. But where twists of fortune and shifts of character in some proffered narration become excessive, we would say to anyone who still wanted to call it one story, that in that case it was a very bad story. Is there a sufficiently coherent canonical narrative to provide us with an 'identity description' of God?

We can approach the problem by way of what may appear at first to be a more straightforward case. The Gospels, we have already acknowledged, are more clearly examples of narrative than is scripture as a whole, and may properly be said to provide us with an 'identity description' of Jesus. Or does one need to say 'identity descriptions'? Ought we to speak of the story of Jesus or the stories of Jesus?[15] It depends on the context within which we are speaking and the degree of specificity with which we hope to give our identity description. For certain purposes and at certain levels of detail, the differences between the identity descriptions provided by Matthew, Mark, Luke, and John are highly significant. But for other purposes, we can legitimately speak of the story of Jesus in the singular. Certainly the church has tried to do so, though not without strain, and in its christological definitions has sought to offer an identity description of Jesus that unifies that offered by John with those which derive from the other three evangelists. If the difficulties inherent in the narrative interpretation of the Gospels in relation to the figure of Jesus are significant, are they not likely to be much greater in any attempt to read the canonical narrative as offering us an identity description of God? Of the many problems entailed by such an undertaking, one merits special mention. If we take seriously, as we should, the apocalyptic emphases in the New Testament, the most natural way of reading the canon as a narrative account of the agency of God involves seeing the story as leading up to an imminent denouement – which did not happen in anything like the way suggested. Does that fact affect the story itself? Or is it to be regarded as outside and therefore irrelevant to, the canonical narrative and its authoritative identity description of God?

What we have to acknowledge is that, even if the concept of reading the Bible as one story is allowed, it is not at all clear what that one story is. The approach may be a useful antidote to fundamentalist and similar ways of understanding the authority of scripture. But it does not make a significant contribution of its own. Nicholas Lash writes in a way that might suggest that it does: 'As the history of the meaning of the text continues, we can and must tell the story differently. But we do so under constraint: what we may *not* do, if it is this text which we are to continue to perform, is to tell a different story.'[16] But that is to restate the problem, not to provide an answer to it. Admittedly Lash has his own account of what constitutes the story and how its essential character is to be determined; it is the 'answer (expressed in the text)' to the 'question to which the text originally sought to provide an answer'. But whether there was one such question and, if so, what it was are themselves questions to which a host of different answers might reasonably be offered. And there is no way of assessing the various possible answers that does not pay careful attention to the work of the critical scholar. The insistence on the need to tell the same story does nothing to rescue the scriptures from the alleged tyranny of the scholar – though it may fruitfully suggest that the scholar needs to be better trained in a wider range of disciplines.

For the writers whose works I have principally been discussing, what is involved in reading the Bible as one story is seen somewhat differently. It is a way of reading scripture to be clearly distinguished from understanding it as historical source.[17] It has its own grounding, whether that is located (as by Wood) in the sense of scripture 'which has become second nature to the members of the community' or (as by Thiemann) in the sense of God's prevenience as it prevailed in an intellectual and cultural atmosphere prior to our own (which he regards 'as an indispensable background belief within the logic of Christian faith').[18]

Such procedures succeed in insulating this way of reading scripture from the acids of recent and contemporary criticism, without having to deny the validity of that criticism within its own restricted sphere. Indeed, the approach can be developed in a way that insures against the likelihood of almost any change of understanding whatsoever. Since Lindbeck regards the traditional trinitarian and christological dogmas as grammatical rules determining correct Christian usage, and since those dogmas are immensely influential in determining how the biblical story is read, even the possibility of any significant change of reading is ruled out in principle.[19] The outcome is a retreat into the ghetto of a world created rather than illuminated by the scriptural text – indeed created by a particular way of reading the text.

I have ventured, in an article in honour of Professor Frei, to react somewhat sharply to the writings of three men all of whose work bears explicit and implicit testimony to his influence upon them. But Frei, as I know to my great benefit, would be the last person to regard theological disagreement as an act of disrespect or a betrayal of friendship. My reaction has been sharp because it seems to me that when narrative is used as the key concept in an attempted rehabilitation of the role of scripture in the church, the result can be dangerously misleading. That is not to deny the magnitude or urgency of the problem these writers are tackling with courage, nor the possibility that narrative interpretation may have a useful role to play in the attempt to find some answer to that problem. It is incumbent therefore on the one who makes such criticism to offer suggestions about how one might best address the problem. This is the more pressing since one of the reasons for Lindbeck's advocacy of a 'postliberal' theology is precisely the failure of liberal theologians to deal effectively with the issue.[20]

I suggested earlier that the main strategy has been to look for some particular form of critical study that will enable scripture to continue to play a virtually unchanged role in the life of the church. But it may be that we would do better to look for a modification of the role expected of scripture in the church than to search for a more congenial style of criticism.[21] The old adage speaks of 'the church to teach, the Bible to prove'. It is this directly probative employment of the Bible that needs to be renounced. It is indefensible, and we ought to be grateful to the critical studies that have released us from its burden and not seek to be 'entangled again with the yoke of bondage' (Gal. 5.1). For the view of the Bible as having directly probative force is not only untenable but distracting. As John Barton puts it in a perceptive article, there are important 'positive aspects of the Bible which are lost sight of as soon as debate begins to circle around the small and sterile issue of whether "biblical teaching" is *binding*'.[22] But does this amount to an abandonment of the idea of the Bible as authoritative at all – and therefore, since I argued that the notion of authority is implicit in the notion of scripture, the abandonment of the Bible as scripture?[23]

'Authority', as we have earlier said, can take many forms, and the word has a wide range of connotation. But its popular understanding is closely limited to the binding or probative role that we are calling into question. Thus it may well be that although the concept is still lawful, the term has become inexpedient. No contributor to *The Myth of God Incarnate*[24] can be unaware of such a phenomenon in relation to our theological vocabulary. Indeed, the abandonment of the use of the word 'authority' in this context has already been canvassed in the church.[25] If we do succeed in extricating ourselves, not only in theory but in feeling, from the sense of scripture as *binding*, and assist ourselves in this difficult task by forgoing the use of the term 'authority', what will be the implications for the life of the church? And what are the uses of scripture that will emerge as important, not on the basis of preassigned roles that it is required to fulfil, but in the light of the kind of resource it is actually proving itself to be?

The first result of learning to see scripture as an indispensable resource rather than as a binding authority will be to help us perceive it better. It is well known how extensively presup-positions and prior expectations can affect what is perceived. The conviction that what we are seeking to perceive has binding authority over us is particularly likely to distort our vision. Freed from that presumption, the church will be better able to hear what the scriptural authors were saying and thus to understand the nature of its own origins. The little glimpses of reality that this will make possible will not always be easy to bear. But in the long run such understanding can only help the church to be truer to its own given character.

More specifically, it will make it easier for the church to acknowledge the varied nature of the stories to be found in the scriptural record, without immediately going on to clip the wings of their invigorating variety in the interest of an already assumed unity. I referred earlier to the way in which the stories of Jesus have come, with the help of agreed christological doctrine, to be read as one story. But the grammatical rules for reading the Christian story (as Lindbeck regards them) have served the cause of institutional control at least as much as the cause of religious truth. For it is not only the diversity of stories that we have to recognize but the degree to which unresolved conflicts and controversies lie at the heart of so many of the writings that make up the New Testament.[26] And having come to a fuller recognition of that, we will be the more ready to acknowledge the continuing presence of diversity and conflict in the later church, not simply as evidence of a sadly fallen later age but as a characteristic of how things are, for good as well as for ill. Thus Stephen Sykes has recently argued in the light of such an understanding of the New Testament that Christianity is an 'essentially contested concept' and that 'Christian identity is . . . not a state but a process; a process, moreover, which entails the restlessness of a dialectic, impelled by criticism'.[27] For if the truth by which we are to live is not authoritatively given in the past but continually to be discovered in the present, such a process of discovery is bound to involve experimentation, with attendant error and conflict.

Theology, indeed, has always been a more creative enterprise than it has been keen to admit. It has sought, sometimes consciously but more often unconsciously, to conceal its originality by presenting its new vision as a restoration, or at least a reinterpretation, of the past. This is a common enough ploy in social and political life, but it has been exacerbated by belief in an authoritatively binding scripture to a degree that has involved serious and unhealthy misperception of what has in fact been going on. Yet a religion of the Spirit ought not to be afraid of creative novelty, even though appeal to the Spirit cannot legitimately be made to justify any particular instance of creativity.[28]

In the last three paragraphs I have tried to sketch a revised context of expectation that might make possible ways of using scripture which would be both religiously constructive and true to critical insights. What form might such uses take?

In the article from which I have already quoted, John Barton lists three positive aspects of the Bible that, far from depending on its being regarded as a binding authority, are likely to function better in the absence of any such attitude. The Bible is (1) the 'primary . . . evidence for the events that lie at the source of Christian faith', (2) a 'collection of theological reflections from the classic periods in which Jewish and Christian faith was forming', and (3) a 'body of literature whose power to inform the lives of those who read it is amply attested in many ages'.[29] In all three respects the importance of the Bible for Christian faith and life is obvious. To pursue the Bible's implications in each of these ways is to deepen one's understanding of this fundamental Christian resource. And since what emerges from such reflection is not to be regarded as directly binding on the Christian, the tension between faith and critical study is less severe.

The transforming power of literature works in any event by its appeal to the imagination and its widening of our sense of the possible rather than by any form of binding teaching. But in the other two respects the revised role being proposed for scripture within the church is more significant. The fact that the earliest theological reflection is rooted in cultural and religious assumptions that we may not share (about, e.g., divine intervention or apocalyptic expectation) becomes less problematic. For that theological reflection is not something we have to take over for ourselves, even in some reinterpreted guise, but is rather something to be used as a resource for our own theological exploration and construction. Similarly, the fact that our historical inquiries leave (and in the nature of the case seem likely always to leave) a large measure of uncertainty about the nature of the founding events of the faith also becomes less problematic. For the precise form of those events is not the heart of the matter. Indeed, the contemporary stress on the narrative character of much biblical writing is not simply a trimming of our sails to the prevailing winds but is in line with the nature of the scriptural sources themselves. Much of the Old Testament, as well as of the Gospels, is historylike rather than historical, not simply in that it has a narrative structure but also in that, while relating to real historical events, it is prepared to redescribe the events with a remarkable freedom born not of any revised historical knowledge but of the revised requirements of the changing experience of faith. Scripture itself can hardly therefore be appealed to as a witness against a similar freedom on the part of those who use it as a resource for their faith.

Nevertheless, objections certainly will be raised against the approach I suggest, and four potential difficulties demand consideration:

1. The uses that I have been describing, it may be argued, do not do justice to the distinctiveness of the canon. In each category – historical evidence, early theological reflection, and transformative literary power – there are other writings that can be called upon, as indeed they are, just as or even more appropriately than some of the writings included in the scriptural canon. That fact must simply be accepted. There are no objective criteria that can justify our treating the scriptural writings as if they were distinctive; to treat them in that way is only possible on the basis of an 'as if'.[30] The particular canon we have received is a matter of contingent fact. But the recognition that its precise contours do not correspond to any set of determinable criteria should not lead us to suggest the abandonment or the modification of the canon as such. The existence of a universally acknowledged set of writings is of proven value, a value that would be free of its attendant disadvantages if the writings were freed of the claim to binding authority. Two illustrations of that value will suffice. In the first place, the existence of an agreed canon helps to provide a common sensibility for the Christian community as a whole; the canon is compact enough to serve that role and also varied enough to relate as a basic resource of faith to the very wide range of human needs. Second, the canon's distinctive status enables it

to stand apart in its historic singularity from the changing patterns of Christian belief, and so to serve as a potential source of prophetic correction over against the ever-present danger of Christians' being carried along uncritically by the beguiling streams of contemporary thought.[31]

2. The approach I have adopted, it may be argued, does nothing to rescue scripture from the tyranny of the scholar and restore it to its rightful place in the ordinary life of the church. Instead it increases the scholar's power by ascribing to him or her not only special skills in relation to interpretation but an innovative function in the form of theological construction also. Certainly the contribution of the scholar remains important. One could hardly expect otherwise, for what the scholar does is only a more concentrated form of what is involved in any reflective reading of scripture – and it cannot be the church's goal to exclude that. But the language of 'tyranny' is out of place. For in the revised account that I am offering, neither scripture nor theology is being afforded any prescriptive role to which the term 'tyranny' might be suited. Scripture and theology are both important contributors to the never-ceasing process of discovering the most appropriate forms of Christian belief and practice. But that is a process in which neither has an exclusive role or any right of veto. For it is a process in which all Christians, out of their varied experience of the life of faith, have a contribution to make.

3. A further result of this approach is that it will no longer be possible for the church to pronounce on some issues of traditional Christian doctrine in a way that it has seemed important to the church in the past to be able to do. That too must be accepted. Similar limits have been accepted many times in the past. A mythological understanding of the story of the Fall in Genesis has made it impossible to affirm a doctrine of original sin which will any longer function as an explanation of the presence of evil in God's world.[32] So the understanding of scripture outlined here makes it impossible to speak of the virginal conception or the bodily resurrection of Christ in the definite way that has been thought requisite in the past. But we ought not to think as if there were a fixed agenda of topics on which Christian doctrine has to pronounce or die. Christian doctrine is the process of making

Christian sense of what the evidence of scripture and experience makes available to us. Doctrine exists for the sake of the church, not the church for the sake of doctrine.[33]

4. Finally, it may be objected that the church will be left with no clear message to proclaim or to live by. Doctrine, it may be said, has been turned into so elusive a phenomenon that it would serve better as the basis for an academic seminar than for a life of faith. But the older approach has always had to face the difficulty of the link between the *fides quae* and the *fides qua*, between the doctrinal content of belief and its effective integration into the life of faith. And on that score our approach may actually have a positive contribution to make. For if the theological task itself, the determination of what can properly be believed, is something that has continually to be discovered in the light of changing experience, then the integration of that belief with life is not a second, distinct activity but an integral part of the process of discovery. The insights of a narrative theology point in the same direction. For the narrative structure of much in the scriptural resource of faith is appropriate to the calling of Christians to enact the story of their lives in the light of it. And the sacramental practice of baptism and eucharist is well adapted to that goal.

The account I have given of the role that scripture should play in the church is similar to that in which James Barr speaks of a '"soft" idea of authority',[34] and to David Tracy's description of scripture as a religious classic.[35] In spite of the fact that my account corresponds pretty closely to widespread practice, I have described it as something likely to be spoken against. That is not altogether suprising if Christianity is itself an 'essentially contested concept'.[36] But there are also the latent guilt feelings that one ought to be ascribing to scripture a 'hard' rather than a 'soft' authority. It is those guilt feelings that I hope to exorcise, so that with fewer anxious backward glances the church can concentrate on the positive potential of the uses appropriate to the present and the future. In particular I have argued that narrative interpretation has a valuable contribution to make to that process, but that if allowed too dominant a role within theology it can have a contrary effect.

3

Newton and the Bible

To salute one's former colleague as Professor of Hebrew with an essay on Sir Isaac Newton might seem a somewhat quixotic choice. But to see it as such is to underestimate the range of James Barr's interests and expertise. Indeed, as the essay will reveal, one aspect of its argument was first brought to my attention by a lecture of James Barr himself.

Newton's interest in the Bible and in theology is well known. The volume of biblical and theological writing among the surviving manuscripts is astounding. Nor was it simply a recreation of his later years, when his main scientific work was complete and his intellectual capacity on the decline. For a number of years, after 1672, that is to say in his early thirties when his creative powers might have been expected to be at their height, it was his dominant concern, largely crowding out any scientific work.[1] The general reaction to these facts has been one of amazement and regret that he should have shown himself such a 'bizarre dilettante in inappropriate disciplines' and dissipated his energies on a study so alien to the sphere of physics in which he had such prodigious talent and success. 'The theological outpourings of the great man were seen' by his scientific admirers in the late nineteenth century 'as aberrations illustrative of the mental weakness that visits even the genius'.[2]

Very little of his biblical or theological work was published. That is hardly surprising. He was extremely reluctant to publish his scientific work; even the *Principia* had to be dragged out of him by friends. And the unorthodox character of some of his theological convictions meant that he stood to lose a lot by publishing them, as his protégés William Whiston and Samuel

Clarke were soon to discover with differing degrees of severity. In Newton's case publication would almost certainly have cost him his Fellowship at Trinity in the earlier period of his life, and his pre-eminent position in society in its later stages.[3] Two works were published shortly after his death, *The Chronology of Ancient Kingdoms Amended* (1728), which he had himself prepared for publication in his last years, and *Observations upon the Prophecies of Daniel and the Apocalypse of John* (1733). The fact that ancient chronology and the fulfilment of prophecy figured so prominently among Newton's theological interests is liable to reinforce any reaction of amazement and regret. We feel as we might do if we were to discover today that some gifted and respected scientist was also a convinced devotee of that fundamentalism which James Barr has done so much to expound and to expose. Such a person is diminished in our eyes because of the intellectual schizophrenia required to hold such divergent approaches together.

But such a judgment, however natural, cannot stand unqualified. Newton's scientific and theological concerns were held together in a coherent unity. He did not confuse the two; he recognized the methodological difference between them. The first of a brief set of seven statements on religion affirms 'that religion and philosophy are to be preserved distinct. We are not to introduce divine revelations into philosophy nor philosophical opinions into religion.'[4] Nevertheless he saw the two as compatible and mutually supportive. 'He shared', say McGuire and Rattansi, 'the belief, common in the seventeenth century, that natural and divine knowledge could be harmonized and shown to support one another.'[5] Nor were his particular theological interests as eccentric as they appear to us at first hearing. Two further recent scholarly judgments may be cited in evidence. 'Chronology', writes Frank Manuel, 'was not a neutral subject circa 1700 . . . The authenticity of the biblical account was at stake and thus by implication the truth of religion itself.'[6] And with respect to prophecy, R. H. Popkin has described 'millenarian theorizing' as 'a most important element in "the making of the modern mind" that can only be ignored at one's peril'.[7] So Newton's theology is worth reflecting on in the context both of his own scientific work and in the context of biblical and theological studies in his day.

Newton himself testifies to a religious motivation behind his scientific work. It finds expression in a letter to Richard Bentley: 'When I wrote my treatise about our system,' he says, 'I had an eye upon such principles as might work with considering men for the belief of a deity and nothing can rejoice me more than to find it useful for such a purpose.'[8] In his view the philosophies of Descartes and Leibniz carried atheistic implications. The idea that life and movement were somehow inherent in matter led to atheism. Bentley, in the Boyle Lectures for which Newton had suggested his name, dismissed the notion as a 'sottish opinion about percipient atoms, which exceeds in credibility all the fictions of Aesop's Fables'.[9] The idea of dead matter, which needs some external force to account for motion, fitted better with the affirmation of God and of providence. So God figures in the Scholium to the *Principia*, where he is described by Newton's favourite term as παντοκράτωρ. 'God', Newton explains, is a relative term, implying Lordship over servants; 'a god without dominion, providence and final causes, is nothing but Fate and Nature'.[10] And in the Clarke-Leibniz correspondence (where Newton's role in relation to Clarke's share of the correspondence has been claimed as 'demonstrably certain'),[11] a crucial issue between the disputants was whether the will of God constitutes a reason for something happening, consonant with the principle of sufficient reason.[12] The Newtonian position was that the attraction of bodies must have arisen from divine will, though it was certainly to be understood as natural rather than miraculous, 'being much less wonderful than animal motion which is never called a miracle'.[13]

Psalm 19 speaks in parallel of how the heavens declare the glory of God and how the law of the Lord converts the soul and gives light to the eyes. And there was a long-standing Christian tradition of the two books, nature and scripture, through which God speaks to humankind. It is a tradition in which Newton stands.[14] For him both books call for a process of careful reasoning if they are to fulfil their intended role of revealing God's story; moreover, Newton insists, it is the same reasoned approach that is required in both cases. This insistence on a single approach to the two sources as the true basis for a reasoned faith is reflected in the series of influential Boyle Lectures, which in the years after 1688 sought to establish the position of a latitudinarian religion over against Deists and Free-thinkers, on the one hand, and the Catholic wing, on the other. Many of the lecturers were close disciples of Newton, and the two recurrent themes are the reasonableness of faith in God argued on Newtonian principles and the reasonableness of scriptural revelation, and its prophecies in particular. Two sets of lectures, given by people particularly closely linked with Newton himself, may serve as examples of those two main themes that characterize the series as a whole: Samuel Clarke's *Demonstration of the Being and Attributes of God* (1704) and William Whiston's *Accomplishment of Scripture Prophecies* (1707).[15]

The book of nature was not an easy book to read. But it was important that people should read it aright. Newton includes among those whose hearts are hardened, who hear and hear but will not understand, 'all they who of how pregnant natural parts soever they be yet cannot discern the wisdom of God in the contrivance of nature'.[16] And he saw himself as one who, under the providence of God, had made a major contribution to the reading of that book. Whiston, indeed, described Newton's discovery of gravitation and the 'wonderful Newtonian philosophy' that stemmed from it 'as an eminent prelude and preparation to those happy times of the restitution of all things which God has spoken of . . . since the world began'.[17] The book of scripture, like the book of nature, was also hard to read. In Newton's view it was 'contrary . . . to God's purpose that the truth of his religion should be as obvious and perspicuous to all men as a mathematical demonstration'.[18] Careful reasoning about scripture was therefore a matter of great moment. And that too was a role to which Newton felt himself called. In the introduction to a writing on the Apocalypse he acknowledges that 'without a guide it would be very difficult . . . even for the most learned to understand it right', and expresses the hope that his book will prove such a guide.[19] Just as the book of nature, properly read under the guidance of Newton rather than of

Descartes or Leibniz, revealed the providence of God in the physical realm, so the prophecies of scripture, read under similarly reliable guidance, revealed the providence of God in the historical realm. Newton drew an explicit parallel between the contribution he believed himself able to make in the two spheres when he claimed that his *Irenikon* 'could do as much to remove the mischief from revealed religion as his other works had done for philosophy'.[20] Nor was this high estimation of his theological, and particularly scriptural, expertise simply his own evaluation of it. John Locke, for example, spoke of Newton's 'great knowledge in the scriptures, wherein I know few his equals'.[21]

What then was Newton's general view of scripture? He did not rate all parts of it equally important or regard its anticipated difficulty as equally present in all its parts. The creation story of Genesis was then, as now, an obvious focus for discussion and dispute. Newton was strongly opposed to allegorizing. He insists to Thomas Burnet on 'the necessity of adhering to Moses his Hexaemeron as a physical description'.[22] But if a defender of a literal interpretation, he is no crude literalist. The language of the creation story, he explains to Burnet, is not in his view 'either philosophical or feigned', that is to say, it is neither scientifically precise nor purely imaginative. To understand it properly, it is essential to recognize how language is being used; it describes 'realities in a language adapted to the sense of the vulgar'.[23] Indeed 'it would be absurd for wise men or prophets to speak to them [ordinary people] otherwise'.[24] So the fact that the account is not scientifically precise is not a defect but an aspect of effective communication. In terms of absolute magnitude the moon is not one of the two greatest lights, but it is rightly described as such in the first chapter of Genesis because that is how it appears.[25] An understanding of how language is being used is particularly important in poetic writings, like the fragments of the Book of Jasher that appear in some of the canonical writings. The poetical expressions to be found there must be recognized for what they are. 'So when the stars in their courses are said to fight against Sisera or the sun and moon to stand still for Joshua, we are to understand nothing more than that Barak and Joshua were favoured by heaven.'[26] The Old Testament histories are human compilations from earlier written sources no longer extant, such as the Book of Jasher. Samuel put together the Pentateuch, Joshua, Judges, and the book of Ruth in this way, and Ezra the books of Kings and Chronicles. Ezra similarly brought together prophecies of Isaiah and Jeremiah, and also the Psalms, into single books.[27] Thus Jewish historical writing is comparable with that of other nations, but also, in Newton's view, superior to it. For though Jewish records experienced the same sort of vicissitudes as those of other nations, they 'have above all others escaped the shipwrecks of time. They have been frequently in danger but by Providence have escaped though not without damage.'[28] One example of such damage is that our present texts may contain scribal errors 'which are scarce to be corrected'.[29] But in addition to their providential preservation, Jewish historical writings are also earlier than any Greek equivalents. Their greater antiquity is important, but not the only or the most significant mark of their difference. They are, says Newton, 'by far the oldest as well as the most authentic being originally written by Moses and the prophets'.[30] However human the process of their compilation, it was the prophetic character of the authors of their now lost sources that gave them their special authenticity. For 'the authority of the prophets is divine . . . reckoning Moses and the apostles among the prophets'.[31] The special authority of prophecy thus applies to a very wide range of the scriptural writings, but it applies with especial force to the most explicitly prophetic works. 'The writings of the Old Testament upon which religion principally depends are those of Moses and the prophets and the prophecies in the Psalms.' The stress which Christ and the apostles laid on them is ample evidence of their pre-eminent importance; and that applies particularly to the prophecies of Daniel.[32] Indeed 'to reject his [Daniel's] prophecies is to reject the Christian religion. For this religion is founded on his prophecy concerning the Messiah.'[33]

In giving such pride of place to prophecy Newton was at one with many of his contemporaries. It was given similar prominence by the Cambridge Platonists, who were also an influence on Newton's early scientific thought. Henry More, in particular, not only wrote an Exposition of the Apocalypse but records discussing it with Newton.[34] Moreover, the political and religious upheaval of 1688 heightened the already existing tendency to relate the fulfilment of prophecy to the contemporary scene. William Lloyd, Bishop of Worcester, and one of the most learned clerics of his day, advised Queen Anne about her conduct of the French war on the basis of his reading of the Old Testament prophecies.[35] But Newton was not simply a passive recipient of the influence of predecessors and contemporaries. His insistence on the importance of prophecy was also an influence on others within his own circle. It would seem to have been from Newton that Nicholas Fatio de Duillier, for a time one of Newton's most intimate friends, derived the concern with prophecy that was to cost him so dear a decade later when his involvement with the French prophets brought on him the public humiliation of having to stand in the pillory at Charing Cross.[36] Once convinced of the importance of prophecy, Fatio found it present everywhere in scripture. He tells Newton that he is 'persuaded and as much as satisfied that the book of Job, almost all the Psalms and the book of Proverbs and the history of the Creation are as many prophecies, relating most of them to our times and to time lately past or to come'.[37] Newton's response to Fatio's enthusiasm is positive but cautious; while expressing pleasure at his strong interest in prophecy, he also expresses anxiety that 'you indulge too much in fancy in some things'.[38]

Newton's cautionary word to Fatio illustrates well the distinctive note in his own approach to prophecy. It was not simply that he would never have risked the social stigma and isolation that befell his erstwhile friend. It was more fundamental than that. Interpretation of prophecy required the use of the same kind of method that had borne such good fruit in the interpretation of nature. 'As they that would understand the frame of the world must endeavour to reduce their knowledge to all possible simplicity, so it must be in seeking to understand these visions.'[39] So Newton's approach to prophecy was a characteristically reasoned one. It begins with observation, which in the case of scripture meant determining the true text. This he pursued with particular thoroughness with respect to the Apocalypse, which he regarded as 'a key to all the prophetic scriptures'[40]. The special authority of the Apocalypse is evidenced for Newton both by its early date, for which he argues by the normal criteria of critical scholarship,[41] and also by the exceptional manner in which Christ chose to give the revelation to John.[42] Newton studied over twenty different versions of the Apocalypse, and two extensive lists of variants are to be found among his surviving papers.[43] When Whiston later claimed that 'a principal source of the mistakes' in Newton's two published works on prophecy and on chronology was due to his 'misguided reliance on the Massoretic text', Newton (had he still been alive) might have disputed the substantive judgment; he could not have denied that Whiston was using against him the kind of scholarly criterion he himself affirmed.[44] Having established the best text, the next step was a careful identification of the prophetic symbolism. This was not something peculiar to individual writers but common to the whole prophetic tradition.[45] Though the prophecies were designedly clothed in obscure form, they were not imprecise or ambiguous in meaning. While it is true in general, as Newton acknowledges, that 'a sentence may be ambiguous', that does not apply in the context of prophecy. There must be a precise meaning to be discovered, however difficult the process of discovery, for anything else would frustrate the prophecies' divine purpose of revealing God's providence in history.[46] The next step was an empirical correlation with important (not minor) events of history. This must constitute a complete explanation of the phenomena of the prophecies themselves, with no loose ends left unaccounted for.

To achieve that goal careful historical work was needed. It was at this point that there was a temptation to rely 'upon the suggestions of private fancy', but Newton is insistent that where scripture needs supplementation for understanding the historical allusions of early prophecy it is better 'to rely upon the traditions of . . . ancient sages'.[47] But there were many difficulties to be surmounted when every detail of a prophecy could be significant and their sequence crucial. Matthew and Luke, for example, recount the same prophecies of Christ but with variation of detail and of order. Newton plumps firmly for Matthew as his guide. Not only was Luke a second-hand authority but his handling of the Sermon on the Mount shows his tendency to reorder his material. Matthew, on the other hand, 'was an eye-witness of what he wrote and had the promise of the Spirit to strengthen his memory and wrote first of any man and seems to keep a good order in the things and relate them entire'.[48] Since we cannot 'say how far Luke kept the due ordering of the sentences and form of expression',[49] he is far less useful to the interpreter of prophecy and Newton is happy in practice to ignore him.

Despite his passionate interest in prophecy and his great stress on its importance, Newton includes in his published *Observations* a general criticism of those who make use of the prophecies to foretell the future. That is not their divinely intended purpose. Their intention is rather that we should trace out the fulfilments of prophecy that have already happened and so come to a worthy apprehension of God's providence in history.[50] Yet Whiston was justified in claiming that this injunction 'is thoroughly confuted by Sir Isaac Newton's own procedure'.[51] Newton's unpublished papers include many calculations as to when the final day was to be expected. The main line of calculation was based on the 1,260 days (a regular symbol for years) to follow the great apostasy. If, as he and the other Protestant interpreters of his time were agreed, the great apostasy was the establishment of papal power, it was not unnatural to take a date around AD 400, thus bringing the time of the end into the late seventeenth century. The precise date could be endlessly readjusted, but most interpreters (especially Whiston) predicted dates in the very near future. Newton, by contrast, tended to give a relatively late date to the apostasy, and, as Whiston noted with regret, could even come up with a date for the final consummation as late as AD 2436.[52] But even when proposing a considerably earlier date than that, the emphasis of Newton's message is distinctive. The date is neither so near nor so certain that it could provide the basis for a clarion call to the sinner to repent and the faithful to take comfort. We cannot be sure of the exact time. As he says, after suggesting various possible starting-points for the 2,300 days of Dan. 8. 14, it may be that our calculation should begin 'from some other period which time will discover'.[53] So while he and Bishop Lloyd are at one in their conviction that the days of papal power are

numbered, they differ in their understanding of the time-scale and
the practical implications of the prophecies. Where Lloyd was
insistent that the country was 'within a very few years of the
beginning of that war of religion which will last to the final
destruction of Pope and Popery',[54] Newton offered a more sober
warning. Even if, as he suggests, 'about 1200 of the 1260 years
have run out', that only shows that there is still time for 'popery'
to increase its power.[55]

With such an approach to the understanding of prophecy an
interest in chronology was inevitable. The two concerns go
closely together. The interpretation of prophecy required a
broader knowledge of history than that which is directly reflected
in the Bible itself. So Newton was concerned to correlate the
biblical chronology with that of other known civilizations. But
such correlation was not only of significance for the understanding of biblical prophecy. As I first learnt from James Barr's Ethel
M. Wood lecture, it also picks up a much older concern to
demonstrate that biblical history reaches back to an earlier time
than that known to the records of any other nation.[56] To that end
Newton is happy to cite a range of indirect evidence. 'The world',
he argues, 'was so thinly populated and so overgrown with
woods before the days of Eli, Samuel, and David that mankind
could not be much older than is represented in Scripture.'[57] But
his main lines of argument are much more precisely chronological
in character. And in that context his firm conviction is that 'the
surest arguments for dating things past are those taken from
astronomy'.[58] That was no new idea, though his own scientific
discoveries had helped to develop the requisite knowledge for
such an approach and it is one that he pursues in great detail.[59]
But the records of other nations are also of great value in this
respect. They can provide historical information not available in
scripture, since 'sacred history constantly passes over all the
transactions of foreign nations wherein Israel is not concerned'.[60]
In general their role is to supplement, not to correct, the biblical
record. Only once does he suggest that they might fulfil that latter
role, when he asserts that the study of profane history provides 'a
better ground for understanding the history of the Jews set down
in the books of Ezra and Nehemiah, and *adjusting* it'.[61]

The outcome of these studies, with their detailed astronomical and comparative chronological arguments, was to foreshorten the traditional Greek chronology by some 500 years and so give grounds for claiming that biblical history takes us back to an earlier time than does Greek history. But Newton's aim was not simply to be able to claim temporal precedence; that claim was part of a much wider vision. He wanted to show how all the religions of the world were corrupt derivations from the original religion of Noah and his sons. That religion, he declares, was also 'the religion of Moses and the prophets, comprehended in the two great commandments, of loving the Lord our God with all our heart and soul and mind, and our neighbour as ourselves . . . the primitive religion of both Jews and Christians and ought to be the standing religion of all nations'.[62] It is a theme that recurs frequently in his unpublished writings. The stress is not on the corrupted character of other religions so much as on the existence of a primordial revelation in which, in the words of McGuire and Rattansi, 'all the truths of God's creation were once revealed as an interconnected whole which comprised natural, moral, and divine knowledge'.[63] These make up 'the essential part of religion which ever will be binding to all nations, being of an immutable eternal nature, because grounded upon immutable reason'.[64] This 'fundamental and immutable' (as contrasted with the 'circumstantial and mutable') part of religion is itself divided into two parts, 'our duty towards God and our duty towards man', which Newton dubs 'godliness' and 'humanity'.[65] The first part has been everywhere corrupted by idolatry (not least in the practices of Catholicism), so that Newton can even assert that 'the Christian religion was no more true and did not become less corrupt'.[66] In relation to the second part, his emphasis is on the identity of the 'ethics or good manners' taught by Noah and his sons, by Socrates and Confucius, by Moses and the prophets, and (more fully) by Christ and his apostles.[67] The distinctive content of Christian belief is acknowledged but played down. Christianity and Judaism are one and the same religion 'with this only addition that Jesus who was crucified under Pontius Pilate was Prince of the Host and head of the Church'.[68] Not many of these more radical thoughts figure in the version Newton prepared for publication with his customary caution, so that the deeper purpose behind his complex chronological computations is somewhat obscured.[69] Nevertheless it is clear that chronology was for Newton a tool which helped to place Christianity in relation to other religions – to the greater glory of the faith to which the Bible bears witness, if not necessarily to the greater glory of Christianity as it had developed in history.

Even if, as I hope I have sufficiently shown, Newton's concern with prophecy and chronology was neither cranky nor purely antiquarian but was intended to serve important religious purposes, there are few today who would judge it to embody an appropriate use of the biblical evidence. Historical providence and the proper relation of Christianity to other religions may still be pressing concerns for the Christian theologian and the Bible may still be a source which has some guidance to offer on both topics, but we would not expect to find that guidance by the path that Newton followed. Just as we have had to learn to read the book of nature differently, so that even though it may still speak to us of God it will not be in the way that Newton laid down with such confidence and precision, so too we have had to learn to read the book of scripture differently. It may still speak to us, but not in the way that it did to Newton. His investigations of prophecy and chronology make good sense when the biblical text is understood at the level of its apparent meaning. Detailed predictions and precise datings are features of the surface text. But a better understanding of the genres of apocalyptic and of ancient historiography suggests that the questions Newton puts to the text are the wrong questions, and that no useful answers will be forthcoming. In relation to those two issues, such a judgment is unlikely to meet with dissent. The difficulty we have to overcome is not that of being misled by his expertise, but rather of finding sufficient empathy to enter into his scriptural world and thereby to recognize how so astute a reasoner as Newton could have pursued that course with such confidence and enthusiasm.

But prophecy and chronology were not the only aspects of biblical scholarship that fired Newton's imagination. He also wrote extensively on christology and early church history. That work never saw the light of day, even in a self-censored form; for it was there that Newton's heterodoxy would have got him into serious trouble. I hope to discuss his work on these topics more fully in another context, and wish to make only one point about them here. His work on early church history was relevant to his prophetic and chronological concerns. As we have already seen, it was needed to help determine the moment of the great apostasy from which the 1,260 days were to be calculated. For Newton that apostasy had a double character, the triumph of superstition for which the papacy was primarily responsible (the general Protestant view) and also the triumph of trinitarianism which was primarily the work of Athanasius (the main emphasis of Newton's earlier writings). The two were closely interrelated, not only because Rome was the aider and abetter of Athanasius, but more profoundly because both in different ways involved the cardinal sin of idolatry – giving to something other than the supreme God the worship that is due to him alone.

But the motive that led initially to Newton's exhaustive study of the fathers was not prophecy or chronology, but christology. Coming to the New Testament text with the same reasoning method that guided his scientific work and his study of prophecy, he was soon convinced that the understanding of Christ it portrayed was of a pre-existent divine reality, fully incarnate in a human life – but a divine reality of a lower status than God himself, the παντοκράτωρ. His approach again involved textual criticism. In a writing entitled 'An historical account of two notable corruptions of Scripture', originally designed for publication in French but withdrawn before the process of publication had been brought to completion, Newton argues at length that I John 5.7 is inauthentic and I Tim. 3.16 corrupted.[70] He believed the same to be true of several other texts – almost all, in his judgment, changed to give a trinitarian sense in the course of the Arian controversy.[71] A careful review of the main body of christological teaching (along the lines that were to find forceful expression in Samuel Clarke's later *Scripture Doctrine of the Trinity*) convinced him that later orthodox trinitarian teaching was at variance with that of scripture. His study of the Fathers was undertaken with the primary purpose of discovering how that disastrous corruption of the original faith, as he conceived it to be, had arisen.

Newton's views on christology find little more support in the church today than they would have done in his own time, had he allowed them to be published. Was his approach on that score, then, as misguided as that which characterized those other aspects of his biblical studies that we have been considering? The general consensus would seem to be that it was not; that in the christological case it was not a matter of putting the wrong questions to the text. For essentially the same questions are still put to the same texts, even if they are made to give different answers. Those texts are, admittedly, understood in significantly different ways and are regarded as less exclusively the determining evidence on the matter; but they are still widely seen as key material in enabling us to assert the true nature of Christ's divinity in relation to that of the Father. But is it right to do so? We have undoubtedly learnt to read the book of scripture in a way different from Newton's, but have we learnt to read it differently enough? It is a question that arises naturally from reflecting on Newton's christological studies alongside reflection on his prophetic and chronological ones, and with it I shall bring this essay to a close. In the light of our changed reading of the book of scripture, could it be that to pose the christological question in terms of the status of Christ's divinity in relation to that of the Father is to pose the wrong question, one for which the biblical texts (when we recognize their true nature) cannot provide us with the necessary basis for an answer? Should christology in that traditional form take its place alongside fulfilment of prophecy and comparative chronology as a subject that belongs to the past history of biblical studies, but not to its present or its future?

Part Two

Tradition

4

Orthodoxy and Heresy

William Frend has not had an altogether wholesome influence on my own development as a patristic scholar. When in the 1960s I lectured on the development of early Christian doctrine at Cambridge, he used to lecture to the same students on the history of the early church. So I knew that they would come to my lectures conversant with the findings of archaeology, alive to the importance of social factors in the life of the church and fully aware of behind-the-scene intrigues at church councils and the eccentricities of some church leaders. I was fortunate enough to be able to take for granted a lively interest in the history of the early church and a proper sense of its practical and human dimensions. So I could concentrate on my own particular interest in the development of Christian doctrine, knowing that my students could supply the appropriate historical context. But if subsequently, and in this chapter in particular, I have continued the habit and have dealt with questions of doctrine with less explicit reference to their historical setting than William Frend would think appropriate, some of the responsibility must be laid at the door of the verve and quality of his own teaching on the subject thirty years ago.

But my tendency to think somewhat too exclusively in terms of a history of conflicting doctrinal ideas is not only a result of that division of labour with William Frend at an early stage in my teaching career; it is also in part an outcome of the way in which the early Christian Fathers saw and presented themselves. It is as a result of that self-understanding, indeed, that the idea of heterodoxy or false belief has come to be integral to the meaning borne by the words 'heresy' and 'heretic' today. The root meaning of the Greek word, *hairesis*, is choice; it means a sect or school, for example of philosophers, who have chosen and follow a particular style of thought or interpretation. It is in itself a neutral term with no necessarily pejorative connotation. In Acts it is used to refer to the Sadducees and the Pharisees (5.17; 15.5) and also to Christians (24.5, 14). But a pejorative note is seldom far away; it is very likely to be lurking beneath the surface when the reference is to a sect or school, which has opted for a way other than one's own. It is clearly present in the one New Testament reference to a *hairetikos*, whom the author of the Pastorals says should be given two warnings before being written off (Titus 3.10). But in that instance it is probably more a matter of a factious individual, who is determined to go and to have his own way, than of someone explicitly committed to a divergent set of beliefs.

By the second century the pejorative sense of the word is clearly to the fore, and so is the intimate link with false doctrine. It is false teachers who are responsible for importing dangerous heresies according to the second-century author of II Peter (2.1). But it is not always easy to tell in such cases whether the underlying cause of division between a writer and those he dubs 'heretics' was a matter primarily of practice or of belief. Ignatius accuses his opponents of docetic and Judaizing tendencies, but in such general terms that scholars have been unable to agree as to whether it is one or two distinct heretical groups that he is attacking. It is possible that their root offence lay more in their challenge to his authority and to that of other emerging episcopal leaders gradually extending their authority over a number of separate local congregations. The Quarto-deciman controversy between Rome and Asia Minor in the middle of the second century over the date for the celebration of Easter was probably sparked off by the practical embarrassment of Asiatic congregations in Rome celebrating Easter on a different day from indigenous Roman congregations in the same city. But it was tempting for those opposed to holding the feast on 14 Nisan, the date of the Jewish Passover, to suggest that those who did so had not properly freed themselves from Jewish beliefs. The issue was serious enough to prompt Victor, Bishop of Rome, to try to excommunicate the Asiatic churches as unorthodox (Eusebius,

Eccl. Hist., V.24.9). The Novatianist schism in the next century centred on the practical question of how to deal with the needs of Christians who had lapsed under persecution. But in the attempts of each side to justify their preferred practice, the differences soon found expression in differing doctrines of church and ministry. Whatever the initial cause of tension and conflict within the church, it was natural enough to regard the real root of the problem as a matter of false belief.

Certainly that was the view that the church came to adopt in the great majority of cases of conflict. And since the heart of the Christian gospel was salvation from God brought by Jesus Christ, it was in relation to the doctrines of God and of the person of Christ that true belief was regarded to be of crucial significance and in most need of careful safeguarding. But before we undertake a survey of how the orthodox doctrines of God and of christology emerged from a series of conflicts between 'orthodox' and 'heretics', it is important to distinguish two contrasting frameworks in terms of which Christian scholars have tended to interpret the evidence which we shall be surveying.

The traditional, 'orthodox' view of orthodoxy and heresy has assumed the essential homogeneity of Christian doctrine throughout its early history. Although the fully developed Christian doctrines of the Trinity and of christology are clearly not explicit in the early stages, they are, on this view, thought to constitute the implicit belief of the main body of Christians from earliest times. Their elaboration into more detailed formulations of belief was necessitated by the false teaching of the heretics, which were deviations from an already known truth, usually embarked on for reasons of personal ambition or intellectual pride. Orthodoxy is always in essence conservative; heresy is by definition innovative.

This way of viewing the general scene has come under increasing challenge. Underlying the older view is a conviction about the unity of teaching within the New Testament. And that conviction comes under great strain in the face of recent biblical studies. The emphasis of such studies is more on the diversity than on the unity of beliefs reflected in the New Testament writings. That there is a broad unity within the New Testament is not in question. Its books are, after all, the writings that were preserved and canonized by the later church with its growing concern for a uniform orthodox belief. But do they represent the full range of early Christian life and thought? The claim that bona fide forms of Christianity were far more varied than even the acknowledged diversity of the New Testament suggests was vigorously presented by Walter Bauer in his *Orthodoxy and Heresy in Earliest Christianity* (first published in German in 1934; ET 1971). Not all of his controversial thesis has won agreement from other scholars. But his main contention, that early Christianity involved many differing styles of belief, is widely accepted. And if it is right, as I believe it to be in its broad outlines, it presents us with a very different framework for the understanding of orthodoxy and heresy. Heresy is not deviation from an already implicitly known truth, which orthodoxy preserves by the process of rendering it explicit at the points under challenge from heresy. Orthodoxy and heresy are rather alternative possible developments of an initially inchoate and variegated movement. Conflicting views can both expect to find support at differing points in the Christian past; and both will necessarily be innovative in developing the inchoate views of their predecessors in the face of changing circumstance and new experience. It is from this latter perspective that I shall be writing; but the former, as we shall see, is the way in which the Fathers themselves understood their own history.

Christian apologists were annoyed to find themselves accused of beliefs that they did not hold and had no desire to defend. They had to acknowledge that some people confessing faith in Christ did hold them, but they were the ravening wolves, the false Christs and false prophets of whom Matthew's Gospel had forewarned them (Justin, *Dialogue with Trypho*, 35: cf. Origen, *Against Celsus*, 2, 27). But despite such strong language of condemnation, Justin can still speak comparatively mildly of those who do not share his belief in the virgin birth of Christ as fellow-Christians, even if badly mistaken ones (*Dial.* 48). Such an attitude, however, was something of an exception and was certainly soon to disappear. No such note qualifies the all-out attack of Irenaeus in his five books entitled *Against Heresies*. The

Gnostics were a more serious problem than a regrettable cause of confusion in the minds of pagan critics. They named the name of Christ, but did so in ways that did not require so sharp a break with the surrounding society and enabled them to avoid the persecution to which Irenaeus' church was subject. Moreover their pretensions to a deeper, saving religious knowledge could serve to entice away members of Irenaeus' flock. The fact that they named the name of Christ did not imply that they were erring Christians. Rather it compounded their error into a form of blasphemy; they were the negation of Christianity, the Antichrist.

But Irenaeus does a good deal more than just pour vituperative scorn on his opponents, more indeed than outline their teachings about God, the world and Christ in a way designed to show their utterly mistaken character. He sets out to show the radical difference between their approach to determining belief and that which is followed by the true church. As their title Gnostic (from the Greek word, *gnōsis*, meaning 'knowledge') suggests, their aim is to achieve knowledge by way of philosophical speculation; the true church follows the contrasting route of faith by way of obedience to what has been revealed and handed down. The primary locus of that revelation is scripture, which the true church accepts in its straightforward sense, while the Gnostics read their own ideas into it by way of allegory. Irenaeus acknowledges that the true meaning of scripture is not always self-evident; it contains, for example, parables whose sense is not immediately or unequivocally evident from the text. But the true church allows its understanding to be guided by the rule of faith handed down under the guardianship of its public officers, the bishops, deriving in line of succession from the time of the apostles; any appeal to tradition on the part of the Gnostics, on the other hand, takes the form of an appeal to the esoteric teaching of a private succession of teachers in the particular Gnostic school.

The logic of Irenaeus' argument made a major contribution to the church's understanding of orthodoxy and heresy. Orthodoxy is that which preserves the true sense of scripture and the original teaching of the apostles. Heresy is a distortion of that teaching, following in the steps of some particular false teacher and deriving ultimately from undue deference to some particular form of philosophical reasoning. Justin (*Dialogue with Trypho* 35) had compared the way in which so many heresies (such as the Valentinians and Basilidians) were, like so many philosophical schools, known by the names of their founders. But Hippolytus, writing in Rome at the beginning of the third century, takes that kind of reflection a stage further. The heresiarchs, after whom the various heresies are named, were not original, creative thinkers. Each of them was dependent on some prior pagan philosopher. Let Christians recognize that link and they will see more clearly what an unChristian distortion of truth the teaching of the heretics is.

Not all those who saw themselves as belonging to the main body of the church were as opposed in principle to speculation as Hippolytus. Origen, the great scholar of the Alexandrian church, also writing in the first half of the third century, was of a very different cast of mind. He was equally firm in his rejection of those same heretical schools that Hippolytus had denounced (see especially his commentary on Titus 3.10; PG 14, 1303b–1306C), but speculative thought, in partial and critical dependence on pagan philosophers, was meat and drink to him. He dealt with the problem by distinguishing between the core deposit of faith, which was handed down by tradition, and other issues, not directly given in that deposit of faith, on which speculative thought was not only permissible but desirable (*De Principiis*, preface).

But the spirit of Origen did not prevail. He himself indeed was to be condemned for heresy three centuries after his death at the second Council of Constantinople in AD 553. His ideas on some issues, such as the pre-existence of souls and the ultimate salvation of all, about which in his view the deposit of faith offered no explicit guidance, seemed to others to fall clearly within a spectrum of beliefs that needed to be rejected as heretical. Even more significantly, with the passage of time the degree of precision that was felt to be required on the central questions of the understanding of Father, Son and Holy Spirit and the relations between them, increased greatly. There too Origen's, often exploratory, ideas came to be regarded in retrospect in an increasingly hostile light.

It was on the topic of the nature of the Son and his relation to the Father that the most important controversy for the subsequent understanding both of orthodoxy and of heresy broke out in the early years of the fourth century. And it is in the context of that controversy, the Arian controversy, that the difference between the two competing frameworks for the understanding of the relation between orthodoxy and heresy is of the greatest importance.

An essay of this kind is not the place for a discussion of the substance of those long drawn out fourth-century debates. The fundamental issue was the nature of the divinity of the Son. That he was divine was not in dispute. But for Arius, and for many other churchmen of the time who did not see themselves as followers of Arius' teaching but who were regularly spoken of as Arians by their opponents, that divinity had to be of a secondary nature, compared with that of the Father. Only so could one avoid affirming two divine principles; only so could one be in a position to affirm a divine incarnation in the person of Jesus, who shared our human limitations and, above all, underwent the sufferings of the cross. For Athanasius and his allies, on the other hand, a secondary form of divinity was no divinity. There was only one divinity and one way of being divine; and if the Son was divine at all, he had to be divine in just the same sense as the Father was.

Athanasius saw the teaching of Arius, and other less extreme versions of a similar tendency, in the same light in which Irenaeus and Hippolytus had seen the Gnostics of their day. It was not a deviant form of the Christian gospel; it was the negation of it. It did not derive from a serious, even if misguided, reading of scripture. Its inspiration lay in Judaism and in Greek philosophy, which for all their difference from one another had in common a monistic view of God, one quite incompatible with God's saving involvement with the world in Jesus Christ. It was an understanding, therefore, that orthodoxy had to repudiate absolutely and uncompromisingly. And so the creed adopted at the first Council of Constantinople in AD 381 (our Nicene Creed) made its point by insisting that the Son is not merely 'God' but 'very God' 'of one substance with the Father'. Athanasius was eminently successful in what he set out to do. For the Nicene Creed, shaped above all as a riposte to Arian heresy, has not only served throughout the church's history as an official touchstone of orthodoxy, but also by its extensive use in eucharistic liturgy has moulded the Christian consciousness at the grass-roots level. And at the same time his perspective on the Arian heresy as a philosophically inspired undermining of the Christian gospel has been accepted, virtually unquestioned, by the vast majority of Christians, almost to the present day.

I say 'almost to the present day' because a very different perspective on Arianism, which has been put forward occasionally by rebel spirits in the past, is beginning to establish itself as the consensus view of modern scholars. This view acknowledges the Arians' motivation to have been as genuinely Christian as that of their opponents. The Arian appeal of scripture was as basic as, and no more arbitrarily selective than, that of the orthodox. Philosophical influence had some part to play in determining the shape of their theology, but the same is true of their opponents. How would it have been possible to produce any coherent and intelligible account of God and his relation with the world without drawing on the best philosophical wisdom their world had on offer? And, above all, both sides of the controversy stood in the same relation to earlier Christian tradition. Earlier Christians had not raised explicitly the precise question which was now the issue of contention between the two sides. Traditional ways of speaking about the divinity of the Son were ambivalent at best; on balance they stood somewhat nearer to that of the Arians than of the orthodox. Either side could, and both sides did, claim with some plausibility that the witness of earlier tradition was in their own favour. But neither claim (particularly that of the orthodox) is as convincing or as decisive as they maintained it to be. Both sides were innovating in a way they were quite unprepared to admit. But on balance it was the Arian heretics who were the more conservative, the orthodox who were the more innovative.

Seeing the controversy this way does not necessarily imply that the Arians had the better case or that there was nothing to choose between the two sides theologically. Indeed some of those who fully accept the consensus, which acknowledges the responsible character of the Arian position, remain convinced that theological right was on the orthodox side – even to the extent of seeing that right as decisive for the truth of Christianity and properly enshrined in a normative, ecumenical creed. But it is not unreasonable to suggest that the changed historical understanding may in time give rise to a changed theological evaluation also.

But the church's decision that the divinity of the Son was 'of one substance' with that of the Father was not the end of the historical struggle between orthodoxy and heresy. It was one thing to be clear that Christ was fully and unequivocally divine; it was another matter to be clear just how that full divinity was related to the human experiences of Jesus. Christians who were at one in their condemnation of Arianism answered that question differently, each side denying the creative novelty of its own view and claiming that its particular position was implicit in the earlier traditions of the church, the only one compatible with the formulas about the person of the Son, already agreed at the Councils of Nicaea and Constantinople. Old attitudes died hard. Episcopal and archiepiscopal opponents might be heretics, but it became increasingly implausible to see them as Antichrist. But the strength of feeling was still there, for the proper resolution of the theological issue was seen as closely tied to the preservation and communication of saving truth. Yet it was closely tied also, as observers were aware then as well as now, to imperial support, and thereby to ecclesiastical influence and power.

The Council of Chalcedon (AD 451), which marked the end of one phase of these christological controversies by ruling out Nestorianism, Apollinarianism and Eutychianism, was nonetheless more of a compromise between competing forms of belief than the councils dealing with the Arian controversy had been. But even so its definition of Christ as one person but two natures failed to stem the continuation of the debate about the person of Christ. For reasons both political and theological large areas of Christendom refused to accept its 'two nature' doctrine and went their own monophysite way. And still further points of dispute arose. Even if Christ had two natures, did he have one or two wills? Monothelites and dyothelites denounced one another as heretics for giving the wrong answer to that question.

The earliest Christians had been taught to say 'Jesus is Lord' and, not surprisingly, to have nothing to do with anyone who said 'a curse on Jesus' (I Cor. 12.2). But who was this Jesus? Some saw him as a purely spiritual being, unencumbered by a real human body. That was judged unacceptable; anyone failing to acknowledge that 'Jesus Christ has come in the flesh' was not of God (I John 4.2–3). But who is the one who 'has come in the flesh'? The early baptismal creeds, forerunners of our Apostles' Creed, defined him as God's only Son. But again the question was asked: What is it to be God's only Son? The answer came back: It is one distinct from the Father, yet sharing in his full divinity without undermining the unity of God. Any lesser account of his divine status was to lie under the curse of the church's anathema. But further questions were pressed: How was this fully divine Son united with the fleshly existence into which he came? And once again any suggested answer which called in question the reality of the integration of the two or qualified the fullness of either or implied a mixing of their distinctive characteristics was judged to put a person outside the true church.

It was a natural enough process and it bears eloquent testimony to the intellectual vitality of early Christianity. But it is hard not to feel that the definition of orthodoxy, of beliefs required of the church and of her teachers, was continually being extended beyond the bounds implicit in the fundamental nature of Christian faith itself. Every movement gives rise to 'heresies', different options which can take the form either of distinct but coexistent schools of thought and practice, or of rival, antagonistic groups each denying the other any rightful place in the continuing life of the original movement. Christianity soon chose the second road. Differences in the articulation of belief were too readily treated as denials of the faith itself. A natural tendency in that direction showed itself from earliest times as Christianity first marked out its own identity over against Judaism and other religious groups in the ancient world. But it was exacerbated by other factors – those personal, social, political and economic factors on which William Frend's work has shed so much light –

and carried over to become the established pattern of handling intra-Christian disputes. The resultant legacy of a well thought out but over-defined concept of orthodoxy has given to the church an intellectual vitality and toughness, but also a penchant for mutual vilification and the multiplication of division, together with a built-in resistance to change in the face of new circumstance.

5

Person or Personification? A Patristic Debate about Logos

One may learn a lot from one's colleagues, as I have done from George Caird, but not usually from hearing them lecture. It is perhaps partly for that reason that I still have a clear recollection of the first of the only two occasions that I heard him give a formal lecture, although it is now nearly twenty years ago. In that lecture, on 'The Development of the Doctrine of Christ in the New Testament',[1] he concluded that 'neither the Fourth Gospel nor Hebrews ever speaks of the eternal Word or Wisdom of God in terms which compel us to regard it as a person'. Our tendency to do so, he suggests, derives from reading those writers in the light of Paul, who, in his judgment, stands alone among New Testament authors in affirming belief in the pre-existence of Christ as a person.

The issue has long fascinated readers and scholars of the New Testament. It is generally agreed that in works like the book of Proverbs or the Wisdom of Solomon the figure of Wisdom herself is to be understood as a personification rather than a person. 'The personified Wisdom of Jewish literature remains from start to finish an activity or attribute of God.'[2] But when New Testament writers make use of the same conception, or of the cognate idea of the Word, do they intend it in the same sense? Or do they envisage a fully personal form of pre-existence? Although (or because) I am on this occasion rashly keeping company with New Testament specialists, I shall not offer a contribution of my own to the continuing debate on that question.[3] I am inclined indeed to think that the evidence may be so ambivalent in character, that no decisive answer can be forthcoming. Nevertheless, however open the exegetical question may be and may have to remain, the church quite quickly gave a clear and unequivocal answer to the distinct, but related, theological question. Modalist interpretations of the person of Christ, which did not involve the concept of a fully personal form of pre-existence, made little headway in the life of the church. The decisive reasons for their rejection had more to do with devotion and worship than with exegetical argument. Nevertheless exegesis did play its part. Our fullest picture of the exegetical reasoning involved appears at a late stage in the debate, when the church's mind is already effectively made up, namely the debate between Eusebius of Caesarea and Marcellus in the 330s. Since this particular exegetical issue is still a live one, a brief account of one aspect of the debate between them may not be without interest.

Marcellus has suffered the fate of almost all those whose teachings failed to find favour in the church. We know him almost entirely through the polemical witness of his opponents. We need always to remember therefore the partial nature of our evidence (in both senses of the word 'partial'). Nevertheless Eusebius cites his words directly to a sufficient degree for us to be able to grasp both sides of the debate with a reasonable degree of accuracy.

The main point at issue between them can be succinctly put. Both believe in a pre-existent 'only-begotten-Son-Logos' who becomes incarnate as Jesus Christ. For Marcellus, Logos is the dominant image and this means that for him the affirmation of any pre-existent personal entity, distinct from the Father, is not called for. For Eusebius, Son is the dominant image, and Logos must be understood in terms of it; for him therefore the distinct hypostatic existence of the Son before the incarnation is of the essence of the faith. Each, as we shall see in more detail later, accuses the other of treating his dominant image too anthropomorphically and thereby drawing false implications from it. Thus the structure of the dispute embodies a classic form of theological argument. If we are to order the varied imagery of scripture in some more coherent way, we are bound to arrange those images in some sort of hierarchical scheme. Some images will be picked out as particularly significant and made the key to the appropriate interpretation of the others. Where one image is so picked out, it will normally be because we believe that it points more directly to and more nearly represents the transcendent reality about which we are trying to speak. A natural retort of anyone wishing to propose some alternative ordering of the images will be to claim that our way of handling the image we regard as dominant is an improperly literalistic one.

One feature in this outline account of the central issue at stake in the debate must be admitted to be problematic. I have said that both Marcellus and Eusebius believed in a pre-existent 'only-begotten-Son-Logos'. But is that true of Marcellus? Did he speak of a pre-existent *Son*? The limited nature of our evidence does not allow us to answer that question with absolute confidence. Eusebius certainly claims that he did not and regards that fact as one of the primary faults in Marcellus' theology that he is determined to expose.[4] Many modern scholars follow Eusebius on this point. Thus Kelly affirms that 'Marcellus restricts the title "Son" to the Incarnate'.[5] The primary evidence on which both Eusebius and the modern writers rely is the statement of Marcellus that before the Incarnation 'there was nothing other than Logos'.[6] But it is noteworthy that when Marcellus contrasts Logos with other titles that belong to Christ incarnate, he never includes 'Son' as an example of that second category.[7] It is thus seriously misleading when Pollard writes: 'He [Marcellus] repeatedly insists that before the assumption of the flesh the Logos was nothing but Logos, and that "*Son*", "Jesus", "Christ", "Life", "Resurrection", and the rest are titles which are properly applicable to the Logos only after the incarnation.'[8] Later followers of Marcellus are quite explicit that the accusation that they separate Logos and Son in this way is one they vigorously deny.[9] So what of Marcellus himself? Other scholars have argued that pre-existent Son is an integral feature of Marcellus' own teaching. Grillmeier draws much of his evidence for such a claim from the pseudo-Athanasian *De Incarnatione et Contra Arianos* and the *Epistula ad Liberium*, which are of very dubious attribution.[10] If we discount this evidence, he can still point to the occurrence of the phrase 'only-begotten-Son-Logos', in the authentic epistle to Julius.[11] It may be that in the letter Marcellus is accommodating his language in some measure to the more general usage of the church. Certainly it seems difficult to see how Marcellus could have remained within orthodox church life to the extent that he did, had he been wholly unprepared to acknowledge 'Son' as a pre-existent title. Moreover he regularly uses 'Father' in relation with 'Logos' when speaking both of God's eternal existence and of his pre-incarnate activity.[12] More significantly in the actual fragments cited by Eusebius there is one reference to the relationship of the flesh to 'his [God's] true Son, the Logos', which seems to show a clear identification of the two not limited to the incarnate state.[13] All in all it seems safest to conclude that Marcellus did not restrict 'Son' to the time of the incarnation, but that 'Logos' was for him so dominant an image for understanding the pre-existence of Christ[14] that the term 'Son' had very little part to play in his own theology. At the same time we must remain open to the possibility that the selective nature of our evidence may be misleading us at this point.

What then are the reasons which lead Marcellus to treat Logos as so wholly dominating an image in relation to the pre-existence of Christ? No doubt the most important is his conviction that by doing so he is enabled to maintain a far more convincing account of the unity of God. But he is also able to give his interpretation a more specifically exegetical justification. That justification is based on the Fourth Gospel. Logos is the title that John uses in the prologue of Christ's pre-existence; when speaking of the incarnate Christ he uses a great variety of other titles, but not Logos.[15] It is therefore clearly the appropriate category for interpreting Christ's pre-existence. Marcellus further insists that in using it for this purpose it needs to be understood in a strict rather than an indirect sense ($\varkappa\upsilon\rho\iota\omega\varsigma$ and not $\varkappa\alpha\tau\alpha\chi\rho\eta\sigma\tau\iota\varkappa\omega\varsigma$).[16]

Eusebius is determined to refute this position on both counts. He marshals a number of ingenious, and sometimes ingenuous, counter-arguments. He does not deny that the fourth evangelist uses Logos in the prologue in the prominent way that Marcellus indicates or that he uses it exclusively with reference to pre-existence. But he points out that it is not the only term used in that context in the prologue. John also employs there the designations of God, light, son, and only-begotten.[17] We have already seen reason to believe that, although this is a serious challenge to Marcellus' more extreme and epigrammatic statement that before the incarnation there was nothing but Logos, it is one which a more measured presentation of his position might not have found it too difficult to meet. Eusebius further insists that these other terms from the prologue (unlike Logos) are also used in the main body of the Gospel by and of the incarnate Christ himself, thus calling into question Marcellus' sharp distinction between pre- and post-incarnate designations.[18] Moreover Eusebius gives a different significance to the distinction that Marcellus had drawn between the prologue and the rest of the Gospel. Where Marcellus had emphasized the difference of content (pre-existence and incarnate existence), Eusebius points to the difference of spokesman (the evangelist and the incarnate Lord). Is it, he implies, right to attach such pre-eminent importance to a title which has only the lesser authority of the evangelist and not that of the Lord himself?[19]

But Eusebius does not, of course, want to deny the validity of the term 'Logos' altogether as a designation of the pre-existent Christ. So he is concerned to reject Marcellus' insistence that the term is to be understood κυρίως rather than καταχρηστικῶς. One objection he raises is that Marcellus' position involves an arbitrary selectivity. If Logos is to be understood κυρίως, why not Son? Since Marcellus' interpretation of Logos is grounded in its similarity to human speech, why does he not similarly interpret the title 'light' on the basis of its similarity to the rays of the sun?[20] As that alleged contrast between Marcellus' understanding of the two terms 'Logos' and 'light' suggests, Eusebius' more fundamental and continually repeated objection is that Marcellus treats the term too anthropomorphically.[21] Sometimes, as when he declares that the divine Logos is 'not like human speech composed of syllables, verbs and nouns',[22] Eusebius uses parody and ridicule to make his point. But it is clear that he is unfair in so doing. Some of his own citations from Marcellus show that it is no crude literalism, but a sensitive use of analogy,[23] with which Eusebius needs to come to terms. And it is vital for him to do so. For he does not appear to dispute that if Marcellus' basic approach were allowed, his conclusions would follow. Logos (in all the various senses that word can bear) exists only in relation to something else; it is not an οὐσία in its own right.[24] When Marcellus says that the human Logos is inseparable (ἕν καὶ ταὐτόν) from the human being, the fault lies not in the statement but in its application to the divine Logos.[25] What Eusebius has to show therefore is that Marcellus' underlying assumptionthat the designation Logos should be treated κυρίως, on a strict analogy with human speech, is to be rejected. And that is no easy task. It cannot be done on any general ground that no imagery is to be taken in that strict way, because Eusebius is himself committed to doing precisely that in the case of the title 'Son'. It is true that the word he normally uses in that context is ἀληθῶς rather than κυρίως. But the two are frequently used together as effectively synonymous.[26] On one occasion, indeed, Eusebius uses the superlative form, κυριώτατον, of the sonship of the only-begotten, and insists that it is this strong reality of sonship, and not any analogy with human speech, which is the key to a proper understanding of the divine Logos.[27] It is not hard to see how easily Marcellus might have turned back against Eusebius the arguments Eusebius uses against [his] understanding of Logos. Indeed, even in the fragments preserved by Eusebius, we have evidence of Marcellus bringing the charge of a false anthropomorphism against the view that sonship implies hypostatic differentiation from the Father.[28] It is not the first time, or the last either, that a theologian has found it difficult to controvert a position he is sure is false, without rendering his own position vulnerable to the same line of argument from the other side.

So far I have been trying to describe the debate in terms of the underlying differences of approach and the broad exegetical justifications of those approaches. But in all exegetical work there is a continual interaction between broad approach and the minutiae of specific exegesis of texts. In this case both interpreters would have claimed that evidence for their understanding of the pre-existent Christ was to be found throughout the scriptures, and in a comparatively detailed and specific form at that. Uncompromising affirmations of the Old Testament about the unity of God might seem to favour Marcellus' cause. But these could be accounted for by Eusebius as temporary concessions to human weakness, like the institution of animal sacrifices, made necessary like divorce because of the hardness of men's hearts.[29] And other features of the Old Testament, like the theophanies, could be used to point in the opposite direction.[30] Moreover Eusebius could complain further that it was a weakness of Marcellus' position that his interpretation of the Logos involved no advance on the Old Testament and would be fully acceptable to a Jew; it failed to do justice to the newness of the New Testament.[31] So it is a long catalogue of texts from both testaments tht Eusebius adduces in his support in the final chapter of Book 1 of the *De Ecclesiastica Theologia*, where he summarizes his appeal to the evidence of scripture.[32] But clearly it is the New Testament that predominates, and the Johannine prologue (its opening verse in particular) that has pride of place within it for the purposes of this debate. Since it is also only there among the New Testament texts to which Eusebius appeals that we have much prospect of recovering Marcellus' more precise exegesis, it is to that that we will restrict our attention here.

'In the beginning was the Word; and the Word was with God; and the Word was God.' Each writer can claim that in each of the three clauses of that famous text, the precise wording and the intended nuance of meaning are evidence in favour of his interpretation. We will take Eusebius first. The phrase 'In the beginning' shows that the Logos has a beginning other than itself. It is not itself ἄναρχος. And thereby it is differentiated from the Father.[33] The use of the preposition 'with' rather than 'in' in the second clause inhibits the use of the human analogy and indicates the hypostatis as opposed to accidental character of the Logos.[34] The same implication is seen in the fact that the third clause describes the Logos as God rather than as God's.[35] Moreover the anarthrous character of the word for God (θεός rather than ὁ θεός) is further protection against any misunderstanding of the phrase as teaching an identity between the Logos and the supreme God.[36]

Marcellus' interpretation is preserved in Fragment 52.[37] He identifies 'the beginning' with 'the Father', since God is he 'from whom are all things'. Thus for him the first clause directly affirms that the Logos is in God, the very conception that Eusebius claims the author has carefully avoided. But the Logos is also 'with God', so that two distinguishable relations of the Logos to God must be intended. The difference is said to be one of δύναμις and ἐνέργεια. That distinction is one that plays a large part in the thought of Marcellus. ἐνέργεια is regularly described as the only category in terms of which one may speak of any separation of the Logos from God.[38] The reason for such a separation is most commonly described as being for the work of creation,[39] though sometimes for the sake of incarnation.[40] It is the former that is explicitly envisaged here, since the later words of the prologue, 'All things were made through him and without him was not anything made', are cited by way of elucidation. The words δύναμις and ἐνέργεια are best translated as 'capability' or 'faculty' and 'its exercise in practice', rather than as 'potentiality' and 'actuality'.[41] In its activity as ἐνέργεια, the Logos does not cease to continue as δύναμις. Thus the first two clauses of John 1.1 indicate the two coexisting forms of the relation of the Logos to God. Finally Marcellus understands the third clause, 'the Word was God', in a way that contrasts sharply with that of Eusebius. The anarthrous character of the word is not commented on, and the phrase is taken to indicate the undivided character of the Godhead.

It is not hard to see how such contrasting approaches to the exegesis of the Johannine prologue could have been carried on consistently throughout. But we do not have the evidence to trace that out in detail. One example from v. 3 must suffice. There the preposition διά is used in describing the role of the Logos in creation. Marcellus appears to have argued that the use of διά supports his less independent, less personal conception of the Logos. Had the author conceived of the Logos in personal, hypostatic terms, ὑπό would have been the natural word for him to have used. Eusebius counters this argument by stressing the mediatorial role of the Logos, and sees the use of the word διά as ensuring our recognition of the Father as the ultimate source of creation.[42]

Neither the position of Eusebius nor that of Marcellus on the pre-existence of Christ established itself as the faith of the church. For while orthodoxy unequivocally sided with Eusebius on the

personal hypostatic character of the pre-existent Son, it eliminated the clearly secondary and subordinate understanding of his
status that was an intrinsic element in the teaching of Eusebius.
Yet it might be claimed that Eusebius and Marcellus represent,
rather better than later orthodoxy, the two basic exegetical
options in relation to New Testament teaching about the pre-
existence of Christ. As the continuing divergence of views among
New Testament scholars today reveals, it is possible to read most
of the relevant texts in either way. In relation to the Fourth
Gospel prologue, for example, on which we have concentrated
here, one modern scholar has suggested a history of the text that
shows the genuine support that both Marcellus and Eusebius
could find there for their particular views. James Dunn, like many
other scholars, believes that there was an earlier Christian poem,
which the author of the Fourth Gospel adopted and incorporated
as the prologue to his work. Dunn believes that in the original
poem 'we are dealing with personifications rather than persons,
personified actions of God rather than an individual divine being
as such'; it is only by virtue of the conflation of that approach
with the Son of God christology characterizing the main body of
the Gospel that 'it becomes clear that for John the pre-existent
Logos was indeed a divine personal being'.[43] If that is a true
speculation we would have a 'Marcellan' originator and a
'Eusebian' redactor of the Johannine prologue. That would help
to account for the way in which both can find reasoned support
for their conflicting views in the wording of that text, and would
also justify the important role given in the debate to the relation
of the prologue to the Gospel as a whole. Indeed this whole
debate about how personally the New Testament writers intended their speech about the pre-existence of Christ to be
understood appears to be one in which the interests and
arguments of the Fathers stand closer to ours than is sometimes
thought to be the case.

6

Eunomius: Hair-splitting Dialectician or Defender of the Accessibility of Salvation?

When I began the study of theology, I did not at first find patristics a particularly attractive branch of the subject. The trinitarian and christological controversies, which bulked so large in those initial studies, seemed to me to be a prime example of those 'strifes of words' (or *logomachiai*, to give them their more forceful Greek expression) against which the author of the Pastorals warns us (I Tim. 6.4). The first step in acquiring a basic sympathy with what was going on in those controversies, essential to any serious engagement with, let alone understanding of, them, was to see how closely they were felt to impinge on the issue of salvation. That is one of the many insights for which I am indebted to Henry Chadwick. So when in my first book I included the sentence 'The concern about christology was not a barren intellectual concern; it was intimately connected with a concern about soteriology',[1] I gave the sentence a justifying footnote consisting of a reference to an article by Henry Chadwick. In that article, 'Eucharist and Christology in the Nestorian Controversy', he not only emphasizes the soteriological rather than psychological nature of Cyril's concern for the unity of Christ, but also brings out how Cyril's eucharistic doctrine 'strikes at the heart of Nestorius' soteriology'.[2] Soteriological concerns were central to both sides of that debate. Few scholars today would enter on any discussion of those fourth- and fifth-century christological controversies without that recognition as a basic element in their approach. Certainly it has remained for me a fundamental principle at the heart of my patristic work.

In recognizing that the principle applies to both sides of the controversy, to Cyril and to Nestorius, Chadwick reminds us of the importance of allowing it to guide our understanding of those who were ultimately dubbed 'heretical' as well as of those who were regarded as 'orthodox'. That has been generally accepted in relation to heretics of what might be described as the theological 'right', men like Apollinarius or Eutyches. It is perhaps not unreasonable to see the latter of those two as an example of someone whose heart ruled his head, of someone whose religious conviction about the way of salvation counted for more than reasoned reflection in a cool hour. But the significance of a strong soteriological concern has been less readily accepted with regard to heretics of the 'left'.

This reluctance has been particularly operative in the case of Arianism. It is not surprising that that should be so. In relation to any of the heretics, our evidence is limited and tends to consist mainly of extracts from their writings selected by their opponents for polemical purposes. Citations chosen with such an end in view are highly unlikely to be ones which bring out any religious or soteriological emphases there may have been in the sources from which the citations have been taken. Recognition of the presence of any such emphasis is therefore bound to involve a measure of reading between the lines, and the interpreter is not unlikely to find only what he expects to find. And in the case of Arianism there is a special reason why people may be somewhat reluctant to find such an emphasis. The Nicene Creed continues to play an important role today, not only in terms of ecumenical consensus but also in the lives of large numbers of ordinary worshippers. Its decisive emphases were shaped by the need of the Arian controversy. It is much easier to justify and draw benefit from its contemporary use if it can be presented as protecting saving Christian truth in the face of a challenge that lacks the essential religious and soteriological dimension of true Christian faith. A vivid illustration of this principle at work can be seen in the Lutheran–Catholic dialogue in the United States. The first document to come out of that dialogue was devoted to 'the Status of the Nicene Creed as Dogma of the Church'.[3] The very considerable measure of agreement reached was clearly helped by the fact that both the main spokesmen, one on each side of the

debate, unhesitatingly accepted the traditional negative assessment of Arianism. The Catholic spokesman, John Courtney
Murray, asserts that 'Arius . . . felt it necessary to appeal to [the]
norm [of the Word of God in the Scriptures], though his doctrinal
system owed nothing to Scripture' (p. 19), while the Lutheran
spokesman, George Lindbeck, claims that the Arian use of the
New Testament subordinationist and adoptionist concepts and
images was heretical, because 'it was opposed, so to speak, to the
intention of the New Testament usage which was to exalt Christ
rather than to lower him' (p. 14). The ecumenical usefulness of
their failure to acknowledge a religious or soteriological dimension to the Arian position is only too evident.

Nevertheless, the recognition of a soteriological motif within
early Arianism is now beginning to find a fair measure of
acceptance in the scholarly world. The book that has done most to
heighten awareness of this issue and stimulate discussion of it has
been Robert Gregg and Dennis Groh's work, *Early Arianism – A
View of Salvation*. Whatever criticism may properly be raised
about some of the detail of their arguments, there can be little
doubt that the perspective suggested by their title does more justice
to early Arianism than Gwatkin's dismissal of the whole movement as 'a lifeless system of unspiritual pride and hard un-
lovingness'.[4] My own work on the *Homilies* of Asterius,
undertaken in collaboration with Robert Gregg as a result of the
stimulus of that book, revealed even more clearly a major
soteriological emphasis in his preaching – more clearly because of
the fuller and more direct nature of the evidence. What is
particularly striking is the different form of soteriology detected in
the two cases. The soteriological scheme which Gregg and Groh
detect in the Arian sources on which they draw is one for which it is
what is 'common to us and to the Son' that is significant. It is the
fact that his sonship is constituted by his obedience to the Father,
by his willing God's will, that enables him to save us into a sonship
in the same mode;[5] whereas in the case of Asterius it is the
distinctive Godhead of the Son that enables him to divinize us by
divine self-giving in incarnation and crucifixion.[6] The two
schemes may agree in finding it necessary to speak of the Son as
divine, but in a sense clearly distinct from the divinity of the Father;

in the one case this is to make it possible to speak of a real obedience of Son to Father, in the other to enable us to speak unequivocally of the Son's undergoing of passion and death. But as schemes of salvation, they could hardly be more different. Perhaps both had a place within the Arian movement, which is probably better understood as a loosely allied group of people with overlapping but by no means identical concerns, held together more by their opposition to certain Marcellan and Athanasian tendencies than by a single specific theological platform.

Plenty of work remains to be done in sorting out the various strands within the early Arian movement and in assessing the true force and character of the soteriological concerns that were undoubtedly at work there. But it is not my intention to pursue that task now. For if most scholars have come to admit a soteriological concern among the motives of early Arianism, the same is not true of later stages of the movement. The derogatory rationalist mantle with which so many earlier scholars clothed the whole Arian movement still sits on the shoulders of the neo-Arian leaders, Aetius and Eunomius. Harnack described them as 'openly proclaiming the conversion of religion into morality and syllogistic reasoning'.[7] And still today the first thing that the student is told about them, at their initial appearance on the pages of a standard text-book such as J. N. D. Kelly's *Early Christian Doctrines*, is that they 'made great play with a hair-splitting pseudo-Aristotelian dialectic, arguing their case in rather specious syllogisms'.[8] The fact that Eunomius was a bishop, even if only for a few months, tends to be greeted with the same kind of incredulity with which a German professor, visiting Oxford at the turn of the century and discovering that the Hebrew scholar S. R. Driver was a canon professor, is said to have exclaimed 'Does Driver preach?'

Is such an account of the neo-Arian leaders justified? Certainly that is how most of our sources present them. There is nothing to match the grudging acknowledgment we find in the case of Arius, that he was a biblical expositor and a man of piety. Nor does a reading of that strange work, the *Syntagmation* of Aetius, with its string of condensed formal proofs of a logical kind, do anything to dispel the impression those hostile sources combine to give.[9]

With Eunomius we have a slightly broader base for any attempted reconsideration, even though in his case too the material comes primarily from the setting of formal theological argument. Moreover, there is one particular saying ascribed to Eunomius which is frequently cited as a point of difference between himself and Arius and as significant evidence of his more intellectualist and irreligious stance. Thus Kelly goes on from his initial scathing account of Aetius and Eunomius to speak of two respects in which Anomoean teaching diverged from that of Arius. The second divergence he describes in these terms:

> While Arius considered the Godhead incomprehensible, the Anomoeans deduced Its perfect comprehensibility from Its absolute simplicity. So Eunomius could claim, 'God does not know His own being any better than we do; His essence is no more manifest to Himself than it is to us'.[10]

Notwithstanding the fact that simplicity was well established as a characteristic of the divine nature, these words cannot fail to suggest intellectual arrogance and the absence of religious sensitivity. Are they valid evidence in support of the traditional evaluation of neo-Arianism? The first fact to notice is that, despite the way in which Kelly introduces the words, they do not come from an established work of Eunomian authorship. They are quoted by the church historian, Socrates, as a verbatim (*kata lexin*) quotation, though without explicit reference to any particular work of Eunomius.[11] Moreover, a very similar sentiment is ascribed by Epiphanius to Aetius, who is credited with saying: 'I understand God as clearly and as fully as I understand and know myself, so that I do not know myself any better than I understand God.'[12] But once again the words do not come from a specific Aetian writing, although a little later on in the same work Epiphanius supplies us with the full text of the *Syntagmation*. They are described rather as the conclusion which both he and those taught by him were misled into asserting, through following out the implications of their initial heretical error. But it is in the more unacceptable form ascribed to Eunomius, in which human knowledge of God's essence is claimed to be equal to God's own knowledge of it, that the saying so frequently recurs in the tradition. Theodoret ascribes it specifically to Eunomius but in a summary account of his own composition, not as a direct citation.[13] Chrysostom and pseudo-Athanasius give a similar version of the saying but in a much less precise form. In both cases it is knowledge of God, not of God's essence, that is said to be claimed, and the saying is attributed simply to an Anomoean.[14]

The authenticity and accuracy of the words ascribed to Eunomius by Socrates must remain an open question. The most that we can assert with any confidence is that there must have been some characteristic feature of Anomoean teaching concerning the knowability of God, which could plausibly be presented by their opponents in this pejorative light. Is it then possible to conjecture what might be the context and intention of this Anomoean insistence?

One proposal has been put forward by Ronald Heine, who writes:

> [The] recognition by Arius that God was incomprehensible gave the orthodox teaching a weapon which, in Diekamp's opinion, was proving embarrassing to the Arians. If one recognizes that human understanding cannot penetrate the divine nature, then one cannot reject the possibility of the eternal generation of the Son having the same essence with the Father. In order to wrest this weapon from the orthodox and to make the Arian teaching secure against their attack, the Anomoean leaders asserted that man can have full knowledge of God's essence.[15]

This account is certainly a plausible one. It represents a pattern not uncommon in the history of theology. If a theologian stresses the mystery of God, it is bound to be more difficult for him to demonstrate that his opponents' beliefs are false. In his desire to exclude what he believes to be false teaching, he is likely to be tempted to claim greater precision (and therefore greater power of exclusion) for his own formulations than the evidence warrants, or even than he himself in his heart of hearts may want to claim. If something like that is in fact what has given rise to the shift in relation to the knowability of God between the earlier and later stages of the Arian movement, we would have to say that the change, however understandable, represents a regrettable narrowing of religious vision on the part of Eunomius.

The evidence of the debate between Eunomius and the Cappadocians certainly suggests that this is the right context for understanding Eunomius' remark, but that the stress needs to be put in a slightly different place. The stress seems to be not so much on 'making the Arian teaching secure' against orthodox attack as on exposing the unacceptable nature of the Cappadocian position. Since those two emphases are so similar, to distinguish between them may appear to be an example of that hair-splitting pseudo-logic of which the neo-Arians are so frequently accused. But putting the matter in this alternative way can help to point towards a more positive evaluation of Eunomius' apparently arrogant intellectualist claim.

It is clear that the Cappadocians appealed to the mysterious nature of the Godhead in defence of their teaching about a co-equal Trinity. They understood both the unity of God and the co-equality of the three persons as data of revelation. *How* the three were one within the simplicity of the divine *ousia* was beyond finite human comprehension. It would not be surprising if some people found difficulty with the claim that there were three distinct persons within the one divine *ousia*, which was agreed to be *haplous kai asunthetos* and regarded an appeal to mystery as too easy an answer to their difficulties. Such an appeal can too readily be invoked to justify any theological proposal whatever. The way in which this objection was pressed home by Eunomius is best understood in terms of the theory of names, which is another distinctive feature of this later stage of the Arian controversy.

Any sensitive theologian must acknowledge the human base, and consequent inadequacy, of the language we use to speak of God. Origen, Arius and the Cappadocians are at one in this. The term *epinoia* plays an important role in the theology of them all. We speak of God not directly but with the aid of human conceptions which enable us to form some notion of God's ongoing activity. Even the word *theos*, the ordinary word for God, refers not to God's nature but, as its etymology was claimed to show, to his oversight of the universe.[16] But what God really is in himself is hidden within the transcendent mystery of the divine being. This approach receives clear delineation in the important distinction between the divine *ousia* and the divine *energeia* which first comes to prominence in this same stage of the Arian controversy. No one gives more emphatic expression to this religiously attractive insistence on the mystery of God's being than Gregory of Nyssa, with his notion of *epektasis*. Even in the life to come, that mystery remains permanently beyond the grasp of finite comprehension. However far we progress in the knowledge of God, there remains a never-ending path of discovery before us as we continue to explore the inexhaustible riches of the mystery of the divine being. No wonder the remark ascribed to Eunomius, asserting his full knowledge of God's *ousia*, sounds contemptible and blasphemous by comparison!

But such a radical stress on transcendence raises a serious problem, with both intellectual and religious implications. If the true God, the God whom it is salvation to know and to be made one with, is, in Paul Tillich's phrase, 'the God beyond God' – the God beyond all that we can say or imagine in speaking or conceiving of him – how can we be sure that our language really does refer to the true God, or, putting the matter religiously rather than intellectually, how can we be confident that we are being brought into living touch with the true God and not with some lesser idol? We seem to be in danger of falling into a Feuerbachian abyss, in which we discover that not only is our language a matter of human invention but so is that to which we believed it to refer. Paul Tillich, whose phrase 'God beyond God' I have just quoted, laid great stress, as did the Cappadocians, on the symbolic nature of all our language about God. He sought to deal with the problem that I have raised by insisting that there is one non-symbolic statement to be made about God, namely that God is being-itself.[17] Although he subsequently modified this claim under the pressure of criticism, he was still anxious to make some sort of comparable claim. Some form of non-symbolic statement (even if in dialectical combination with the symbolic) continued to be regarded by him as vital to the intellectual and religious coherence of his whole scheme. 'It is the condition for man's religious existence and for his ability to receive revelation.'[18]

May not something similar be a significant concern in the case of Eunomius also? Certainly he castigates the Cappadocian understanding of language about God as untrue to scripture and involving a reduction of it to a form of human invention that renders it unable to fulfil its goal.[19] This might be just one more indication that Eunomius does not belong to the category of 'sensitive theologian' to which I referred earlier. But Eunomius is no crude literalist. He has no intention of denying that words when applied to God have to be understood in an appropriately divine sense and do not mean the same as when applied to earthly realities.[20] But that does not give the interpreter licence to understand them as he or she will. The relation of words to things is given by God.[21] And in some cases those words relate directly to the essence of that which they indicate.[22] This more realistic theory of language is important to Eunomius, to ensure that there is an identifiable referent for the language we use and that the language really does apply to it. As Richard Vaggione argues: 'The purpose of his language was surely not to claim an exhaustive knowledge of reality, but to make a knowledge of reality possible at all by guaranteeing the objective reference of words.'[23]

If this is a valid interpretation of the general concern inherent in Eunomius' theory of language, then his notorious remark about the measure of his knowledge of God is likely to have been more limited in scope and patient of a more religious significance than his opponents allow. Eunomius, for his part, taunted them with worshipping what they do not know, like the Samaritans of old (John 4.22),[24] something incompatible, he says, with claiming the name of Christians.[25] That is certainly a polemical parody. But so, surely, is their understanding of his contrasting position as a claim to equality with the divine self-knowledge. It is most unlikely that Eunomius was claiming to know all that there is to be known about God. It is much more likely that he was simply claiming to know enough about the *ousia* of God, about what it is to be God, to be able to exclude what he regarded as Cappadocian mystification and to ensure that our Christian language refers, that our speech about God has a purchase on reality.

The point can be expressed in soteriological terms, which reveal a rough similarity to the soteriological issues at stake in the christological controversies which I referred to at the outset. There the two principles involved were that the one who saves must be fully divine, since only the fully divine can be the author of salvation, but he must also be one with us, so that salvation can be effectively received.[26] Different schools varied in the effectiveness of the emphasis they put on the two sides of this dual requirement. The church struggled to hold the two together, but never succeeded in doing so fully without strain and conflict. So in this debate one might say that the object of human worship must be radically transcendent because only the fully transcendent is worthy of worship, but must also be available as an object of our real knowledge so that the worship can be properly directed. Eunomius, I want to suggest, was genuinely concerned that the Cappadocian stress on transcendent mystery had lost its hold on that second important soteriological, or perhaps in this context one might better say doxological, principle.

Even if in this kind of way Eunomius' claim can be made to appear less bombastic than it is usually understood to be, the claim is still there and we need to ask what it amounts to. What is the content of this claimed knowledge of the divine *ousia*? It is usually asserted that the fundamental claim that Eunomius wants to make about the divine *ousia* is that it is *agennētos*. That God is the unbegotten is taken to be the crucial non-symbolic statement that Eunomius is determined to make about God, and unbegottenness the true and literal description of what God is. And the fact that it is so philosophical a term which is assigned this crucial role is seen as further evidence of the precedence of the rational over the religious in Eunomius' concerns. But considerable caution is needed at this point. The use of the term *agennētos* to refer to God was no novelty, introduced at a late date into Christian discourse. It was traditional Christian usage of two centuries' standing. Its particular centrality in the thought of Eunomius is certainly evident from the major role it plays in the *Apologia*. Moreover it is unquestionably true that in his controversy with Basil, Eunomius is keen to insist that unbegottenness characterizes the divine *ousia* as such and not just the hypostasis of the Father. The point is vital to his argument with his opponents, and if it is once granted he has an unassailable advantage in the ensuing debate with them. The status of the term *agennētos* is therefore the issue most extensively discussed. Nevertheless, if we isolate that term and see it as providing the primary designation of God in the thought of Eunomius, I believe we are in danger of building up a misleading picture of the underlying character of his theology. It is not *agennēsia*, I want to suggest, that he is tempted to regard as the proper name for God.

The denial that God has a name was well established, both inside and outside Christianity, as a way of emphasizing God's transcendence. It is strongly asserted by Justin, who says that the reason God cannot be named is the fact that he is *agennētos*. 'Father', 'God', 'Creator' and such like terms are not strictly names (*onomata*) but forms of address (*prosrēseis*) derived from divine activities.[27] That particular linguistic distinction can hardly be observed consistently in the light of the use of the word *onoma* in scripture. Thus in another, baptismal, context where Justin again asserts the impossibility of naming the ineffable God, he cannot avoid speaking of the 'name of the God the Father and Lord of the Universe' in which the believer is baptized.[28] But his proposed distinction between *onoma* and *prosrēsis* is a way of drawing attention to the variable status of different names or designations, a point of great significance in later discussion. Origen held a high doctrine of the significance of names. They are not, for him, a matter of arbitrary convention, but have an intrinsic relation to the things they describe. It is therefore important that we use the proper names for God, and that means the names given in scripture.[29] On more than one occasion he cites Exodus 3.14 in a form which gives God's words to Moses as: '*ho ōn*, that is my name'.[30] And in his discussion of the clause in the Lord's Prayer, 'Hallowed be thy name', he argues that since God is unchanging so must his name be. He allows that there might be more than one name, provided they all carry the same signification, but the one name that he selects to give (recalling its scriptural source) is *ōn* – being or being-itself.[31]

Origen's discussion (with its assertion of a theory of language akin to that of Eunomius) provides a clue to what may lie at the heart of Eunomius' position. The same text, Exodus 3.14, is of central importance to Eunomius also. It is a recurrent theme in the surviving literary debate between Basil, Eunomius and Gregory.[32] Moreover, in the *Apologia* itself, it is one of two scriptural examples which Eunomius selects to illustrate words that directly refer to God.[33] It is surely more probable that Eunomius should have regarded the scripturally given *ōn* rather than *agennētos* as constituting the true name of God.[34] It is, of course, closely linked with *agennētos* in Eunomius' thought. For Origen it is the unchangeableness of being that is its most fundamental aspect. Thus in his discussion in the *De oratione* it is the terms *atreptos* and *analloiōtos* that are most directly linked with the designation of God as *ōn*. For Eunomius it is the underivedness of being that is most significant, and therefore the term *agennētos* that is most intimately associated with it. *Agennētos* is indeed affirmed to be descriptive of the divine *ousia*. But Eunomius goes on to insist that such a description is to be understood as a way of fulfilling our fundamental duty to 'confess that he is what he is'. Even though the words do not take the form of a direct quotation of Exodus 3.14, the phrase is most naturally to be taken as involving a specific allusion to it. For Eunomius, insistence on *agennētos* as characterizing the divine *ousia* is a way of spelling out what is implicit in the fact that God's name is *ōn*.[35]

But Basil will have none of it. *Agennētos*, he argues, can come no nearer to expressing what God is than can a physical term, like fire; it can express only how God is.[36] But it is not only Eunomius' understanding of *agennētos* that he challenges. He also takes him to task for his interpretation of Exodus 3.14 and denies that it shows *ōn* to be the name of God. In the first place, he argues, the name in view in the passage is the immediately preceding 'God of Abraham, God of Isaac, God of Jacob' and not the earlier 'I am'. And, second the name envisaged is not the name of God's essence; that, as Exodus 6.3 implies, remains unrevealed.[37] Here, too, there is a point of fundamental divergence, perhaps the most fundamental point of divergence, between Eunomius and his opponents. For Eunomius, being or reality (*ōn*) is God's name;

for his opponents the really real (*to ontōs on*) is above every name.[38]

To call God 'being' or 'being-itself' sounds to many contemporary ears as discouragingly philosophical in character as to designate him 'unbegotten'. Certainly that objection was vigorously raised against John Robinson's use of 'ground of being' in *Honest to God* (SCM Press 1963). But for Eunomius the term came with the sanction of scripture (and God's self-designation in scripture at that), as well as with the support of a long-standing tradition. He had good grounds for rejecting any suggestion that he was replacing Christian language with the language of philosophy. Indeed, in his eyes it was precisely his opponents of whom that was true. It is to claim that God is beyond being, he could argue, that is to succumb to the influence of Platonic philosophizing; to call him being is to stay with scripture and revelation.

Is there any wider evidence that might offer support to this more religious interpretation of Eunomius' basic position? The proposal as outlined so far is a highly tentative one. The nature of the material from Eunomius' own pen, as well as the citations in polemical sources, is singularly ill-suited to reveal any deeper religious concerns. The difficulty of drawing on other sources by way of corroboration is that the Eunomian provenance of other writings cannot itself be more than a matter of conjecture. But it is worth drawing attention to two other writings, the *Clementine Recognitions* and the *Apostolic Constitutions*, although it would require a much more detailed discussion than is possible here to make use of them in anything more than a highly tentative way.

Of the two, the *Clementine Recognitions* is the better established as a potential source of Eunomian teaching.[39] One section (III.2–II) is widely acknowledged to be an interpolation of Eunomian provenance. In general character it is not very promising material for our purpose, but Vaggione points to two passages in that interpolation relevant to our theme.[40] 'Unbegotten' is there stressed as a fundamental attribute of him who is. But it is a human designation indicating that God is without beginning, not made or begotten even by himself. It does not tell us what God is. That is known only to God himself.[41] This might

be seen as a correction from within the neo-Arian movement itself
to the more extreme claim ascribed by Socrates to Eunomius. It
makes very much the same point that Basil makes against
Eunomius, despite the fact that the passage as a whole is clearly
Eunomian in character.[42] On the other hand, it may be a more
accurate presentation of Eunomius' own position than the strong
version of it assumed by his opponents for polemical purposes.
Mme Harl speaks of 'la distinction, si souvent reprise chez les
pères Grecs, entre savoir que Dieu existe et pouvoir definir son
ousia: le titre *ōn* renvoie a cette *ousia* divine sans le definir'.[43] It
would not be surprising if there were confusion and misunderstanding in the drawing of this distinction. To insist that *ōn* is a
name for God, correctly describing the divine *ousia*, need not ever
have been intended to suggest a definition of God, in the sense of a
full knowledge and comprehension of what God is. It may rather,
as I have been suggesting, have been intended as a means of
ensuring that the God whom we claim to know is real, or better
the real, and not a figment of the imaginative power of human
words. The *Clementine Recognitions* cannot be used to clarify
the issue with any confidence. But they do seem to offer some
support, however tentative, to the argument already developed
that the Anomoean position did not lay claim to an exhaustive
knowledge of God in the way its opponents allege.

Since Vaggione's thesis was written, Thomas Kopecek has
given further support to the identification of the final redactor of
the *Apostolic Constitutions* as neo-Arian, with the promise of a
fuller statement of his case in the future.[44] In the liturgies of
Book VIII, God is addressed as *agennētos* at a number of the
most solemn points in the liturgy.[45] However philosophical the
word's origins, it is here integrated into the stuff of worship.
There is nothing surprising in that. *Homoousios* entered Christian vocabulary as a result of theological controversy, in a way
which required even those who most strongly supported it to
offer somewhat embarrassed apology for its unscriptural tone.
Yet 'of one substance' has become a focal point of devotion in the
recitation of the Creed and 'consubstantial' can stand with
powerful effect in the doxologies of hymns. Read one way, the
liturgies of the *Apostolic Constitutions* can sound like highly

artificial and undevotional constructions; read another way, they can provide an impressive evocation of awe in the presence of the divine majesty. One incidental feature of these liturgies is particularly pertinent to our discussion. The opening words of the long prayer for the ordination of a bishop are *ho ōn*.[46] In this solemn prayer it is *ho ōn*, rather than *theos* or *kurios* or *patēr*, which is the initial form of address to God. That term for the neo-Arians was not only philosphically important. It came to them with the force of scripture and tradition as well. It combined the connotations of 'being-itself' and 'the Great I am'. It was for them the primary name of God, given by God himself and serving to ensure that our worship is directed to the true God, to God as he really is. It could be used not only in talk about God, but in address to God.

It has not been possible in a single paper to discuss every aspect of Anomoean faith or practice – indeed, I have not touched at all on many of those areas, such as christology, baptism or eucharist, which have most obvious links with the theme of salvation. I have chosen to look rather at the issues of debate for which the neo-Arians were most strongly criticized at the time and which have been the basis of subsequent evaluation of them as even more unspiritually minded logic-choppers than Arius himself. And I have ventured to claim that even there it is not unreasonable to see a deeply felt religious and soteriological concern – how to affirm the true and transcendent God in such a way that we may know him and worship him as he really is. Knowledge of the true God has an intellectual dimension, but it is not an exclusively intellectual matter; it is essential to worship in spirit and in truth. And it is essential to the way of salvation, since it is knowledge of the only true God which is life eternal (John 17.3).[47] To present the arch-heretic, Eunomius, in such a light is not to ask for a reversal of the judgment made in favour of Cappadocian orthodoxy. It is only to insist that, even in this most unpromising of cases, the line between orthodoxy and heresy is not the line between a soteriological and a rationalist concern, between a religious and a philosophical spirit. Rather, it is a line which separates two understandings of the faith, both of which were equally concerned to offer a reasoned faith as a way of salvation.

Part Three

Reason

7

On Being a Theologian in Today's Church

My first visit to the Netherlands was in 1977, to speak to an ecumenical group about a recently published Church of England Doctrine Commission report, *Christian Believing*.[1] The first question after I had spoken was one that took me by surprise. 'How', asked the questioner, 'could you have produced a report that sounds so like an after-dinner discussion in an Oxford Common Room, and has nothing to say about praxis or about Marxism?' The questioner, then unknown to me personally, was Gerard Rothuizen. It was the beginning of a much valued friendship, in which discussions of how we should be doing our theology today have often played their part. In one respect they have been lopsided discussions. For while he has read and commented with a kindly but critical eye on much that I have written, my ignorance of the Dutch language has prevented me from reciprocating in relation to his own published work. So it seems appropriate that I should contribute to this volume in his honour some reflections on the role of the theologian, who seeks to make a critical but constructive contribution to the life of the church.

'Would that all the Lord's people were prophets!', declared Moses (Num. 11.29). It was an unexpected response to those who had told him in shocked tones that Eldad and Medad were prophesying in the camp, where they had stayed instead of joining him, their acknowledged leader, at the appointed tent of meeting. One may admire the spirit of Moses' reply, while still having doubts as to how beneficial it would have been, had his wish been granted. If today one were to express the hope that 'all the Lord's people were theologians', many would be likely to respond with the words so frequently used by St Paul – 'God forbid'. Yet in one sense all (or virtually all) the Lord's people already are theologians. For if to be a theologian is (as the etymology of the word suggests) to be someone who seeks to speak in a reasoned way about God, most Christians have done that to some degree at some time. Just as Molière's M. Jourdain was surprised and delighted to discover that all his life he had been speaking prose without knowing that that was what he was doing, so many a Christian will be surprised (if not necessarily delighted) to learn that he or she over the years has done a good deal of theology without realizing it. That does not, of course, invalidate the fact that some people are called to be theologians in a more specialized sense. But it is an important reminder of the context in which they do that theology. Just as the priesthood of all believers does not rule out the calling of some to be priests in a special sense, but should rule out the idea that the priest is a different kind of person doing different kinds of things from those which concern the laity, so too with the theologian. He or she has a special responsibility to do something in which every one of us, however falteringly, is also engaged.

In using the word 'theologian' in the title of this essay, it is in the more specialized sense that I intend the word to be understood. Indeed, my intended sense is narrow enough to exclude even the biblical scholar and the church historian (indispensable though their contributions are to the work of the theologian). By theologian I mean someone whose special task it is to talk, not about other people's beliefs about God, past or present, but to talk about God – and to do so in a way that can be commended to others as coherent, as reasonable, as true. What an audacious role to undertake! No wonder that in the past theologians have so often claimed that some clear-cut and decisive authority is available to us in the text of the Bible or in the teaching magisterium of the church. Would he not be a monstrous egomaniac if he did not seek to base himself on some authority other than himself in that sort of way? Yet it is just that kind of an appeal to some decisive external norm, which has characterized so much theology in the past, that in my judgment is no longer possible. There are, of course, still those who would go on maintaining that some such form of absolute authority is available to us. I am not going to argue the case against them here; that has been done often enough and my reasons for rejecting any such approach will emerge clearly enough in the course of the essay. I propose to begin instead by simply assuming that such an approach is not a serious possibility for us, and attempt what I hope will prove the more constructive task of asking what alternative is open to us in the face of that impossibility.

To what authority can the theologian appeal? By what authority does he operate? 'By what authority?' That question was one that was put to Jesus. Let me begin by recalling the incident, as Luke's Gospel describes it:

> One day as Jesus was teaching the people in the temple and preaching the gospel, the chief priests and the scribes with the elders came up and said to him, 'Tell us by what authority you do these things or who is it that gave you this authority' (Luke 20.1–2).

Christians customarily think of the authority of Jesus as bound up with his unique status and therefore different in kind from that of any subsequent Christian teacher. It might therefore seem either irrelevant or presumptuous (or possibly both) to begin a consideration of the theologian's authority from this story of the same challenge directed to Jesus. But Jesus' answer to the question suggests that it may not in fact be as inappropriate as it might at first sight appear. For Luke's account continues:

> He answered them, 'I will also ask you a question; now tell me, was the baptism of John from heaven or from men?' (vv. 3–4).

Unless Jesus' counter-question about John the Baptist is sheer evasion it implies that there is some significant similarity between the authority for his own activity and that of John. So I am encouraged to claim that an approach to our question by way of some reflections about the authority for the teaching ministry of Jesus may in fact be legitimate and potentially fruitful.

Jesus was a Jew. It was his custom to attend synagogue. Despite the seriousness of his conflict with the religious authorities of his day, he did not dissociate himself from the religious life of his people. The Old Testament scripture and the ongoing life of Judaism were vital constituents of his spiritual formation. But his stance in relation to them was a critical one. The explicit provisions of the Mosaic law about divorce could be challenged on the basis of the broader vision of the creation story: 'It was for the hardness of your heart that Moses wrote you that commandment. But from the beginning of creation God made them male and female, and for this reason a man shall leave his father and mother and be joined to his wife and the two shall become one.' Other provisions of the law and of the tradition could be countermanded or extended in the light of his own religious vision. 'You have heard that it was said to the men of old . . . But I say to you . . .' For there can be little doubt that the controlling factor in his teaching was a personal vision, growing out of but not wholly determined by the tradition in which he had been nurtured. The parabolic form of his teaching was much more than a species of sermon-illustration; it was integral to the teaching, because it was integral to the creative vision that gave rise to it. And the purpose of the teaching could only properly be grasped by those who had been enabled to share that vision. 'He who has ears to hear, let him hear!'

Something of the same structure can be seen in the work of literary interpretation. Most literary critics are unwilling to speak of *the* meaning of a text; they reject the idea that a work of literature has one and only one meaning. But if we allow for a plurality of meanings, the question that naturally arises is: Are there any limits? How do we distinguish between good and bad, between valid and invalid interpretations? There is obviously no rule of thumb method by which such discrimination can be effected. But some guiding principles can be enunciated. An interpretation is to be taken seriously if the one who proffers it is someone who is steeped in the tradition to which that piece of literature belongs, if he has given to it not just a passing glance but sustained and critical attention, and if his interpretation once put forward speaks to others who are prepared to share in the same serious quest for understanding.

Three features of that account are closely parallel to the picture that I have drawn of Jesus: belonging to a tradition; a serious and critical wrestling with the tradition; and an offering for the judgment of others of the vision resulting from that wrestling. Those three features, I want now to suggest, are the essential marks of an authentic theologian with a proper authority to speak. And it is the implications of stressing those three things as the basic ingredients in the undertaking of the theologian's task that I propose to draw out.

1. My first feature was belonging to a tradition. For the Christian theologian that means that the church is the context within which his or her theology needs to be done. He will not always feel at ease there, but that is the place where he needs to be. Edward Schillebeeckx, who has certainly not always been allowed to feel at ease in his church, declares that 'without the church my quest would never have arisen'; and goes on to speak of the church as a 'theological habitat' without which the theologian's reflections have nothing to ground themselves upon.[2]

Perhaps, however, 'church' is too formal and too institutional a term for that which seems to me to be vital. Karl Rahner describes 'the true basis and the ultimate prior condition for . . . an ecumenical theology' as constituted by 'a faith which we hold in common at the heart and centre of our lives' on both sides of the ecumenical dialogue.[3] It is serious commitment, not necessarily to a specific institutional body, but in some form or another to the community of faith, that is vital. And it is vital because that community is the living conveyor of the tradition, which is the matrix out of which any theology demanding our attention has to come. And why should it be so important that the theologian belong to that tradition? Because, although the theologian's task is to speak to the present, if his attention is limited to the present, what he has to say is sure to be superficial. Only someone who is well-versed in scripture and in the history of the tradition in which he stands is in a position to speak with any authority in relation to the present.

This first feature that I regard as an inescapable requirement of a serious theologian corresponds up to a point to the traditional emphasis on the authority of the Bible or of the ecumenical creeds

or of the teaching magisterium of the church. Appeals to *those*
sources of authority have, as I have already indicated, usually
been made in the past in an absolutist form that I regard as no
longer defensible. Revelation is not accessible in the pure,
untainted form that such claims presuppose. What I believe the
Christian theologian *is* committed to, and must be committed to
if he is to function as a Christian theologian at all, is not that there
are isolable or unquestionable truths of revelation to be found at
some point in the tradition, but that there is vital truth about God
to be learnt there that is not to be found elsewhere. I do not claim
that he must believe that there is vital truth about God to be learnt
there and there only; he does not need to make the claim that his
Christian sources are the sole avenue to divine truth. But he must
believe that there is vital truth about God to be learnt there that is
not to be found elsewhere. He does *not* need to make a claim to
exclusive truth, but he *does* need to make a claim to distinctive
truth.

2. I have been stressing that the theologian must be committed
to the Christian community and well-versed in the Christian
tradition – but that is not the same as to say that he must be
uncritical of either. True loyalty always involves readiness to
speak the unwelcome truth in love. Certainly continuity of the
church's life and tradition is a matter of great importance. All that
I have said so far about the need for the theologian to be
committed to the community and well-versed in its traditions
witnesses to the fact that continuity is something about which he
must be concerned. But that continuity is not a matter of theology
alone; it is a matter of the whole life of the church in its worship
and in its practice. A formal church structure is indispensable not
merely for the bare fact of the continuity of the church's
existence, but also for the nurturing of the lives of its members
and the furtherance of genuinely personal life within it. Such
formal structure requires persons responsible for its preservation,
but the theologian is not one of those whose *primary* concern lies
there. The structures of institutional life, indispensable though
they are, have a built-in tendency towards ossification and
restrictiveness. But to live is to change, and for the stimulation of
such a change a prophetic voice is needed. And it is there that the

theologian has a special task to fulfil. For his primary concern is with the task of the appropriate adaptation of the church's patterns of thought and belief down the ages. And that is a never-ending task. It is never-ending for two reasons. It is never-ending in the first place because of the inadequacy and indirectness of our human language. Catholic Christianity has always stressed the incompetence of human speech to give adequate expression to the transcendent realities of God's truth. It has not always been so ready to stress the implications of that proper insight which point to the inevitably provisional character of its own forms of speech about God. And it is never-ending in the second place because of the impact of historical change. What the Christian community can properly say about God is rooted in the community's experience of God in the world. And any major shift in our knowledge and experience of the world has subtle repercussions on what we can properly affirm about the nature and activity of God. A concern to discover the appropriate adaptation of our forms of belief in the face of an always changing environment of that kind is a difficult and dangerous task. In the report of the Church of England Doctrine Commission, *Believing in the Church*, that was a sequel to the one to which I have already referred, the church historian, John McManners, uses a military metaphor. 'The church', he says, 'needs snipers outside the main trenches, free from all responsibilities except loyalty to the cause, and picking off the enemy at their discretion . . . It is unsettling to some Christians to find "dangerous" theories aired and, what is worse, greeted with suspect enthusiasm by unbelievers. Yet living dangerously is, after all, the only way of living intensely. The truth that makes us free is found only by the exercise of freedom. As Christians, we have to get used to being totally committed to a faith which can only be provisionally stated.'[4] If, as I have suggested earlier, those who bear responsibility for the pre-servation of the church's organizational life are necessary but dangerous – necessary because such preservation is vital, but dangerous because always tempted to achieve it by the easy but false way of being excessively restrictive of change, so too is the theologian, though in precisely the opposite respects – necessary as agent of necessary change, but dangerous because the changes that he or she proposes may in fact be pointing in quite the wrong direction.

If this kind of activity is (whatever its risks) essential to the continuing discovery, and thereby the maintenance, of truth, how is the theologian to address himself to it? I said earlier that the church was the place where the theologian needed to be, the context within which his theology needs to be done. The American Roman Catholic theologian, David Tracy, has distinguished three different publics, which may serve to determine the pattern of a theologian's work: society at large, the academy and the church. But in the end, he argues, the three cannot and ought not to be kept apart. In the long run the theologian needs to speak, in Tracy's phrase, with 'responsibilty for authentically public discourse',[5] that is to say, in a way that is relevant to every aspect of human life and not just to the narrower ecclesiastical circle. Certainly when I spoke of the church as where the theologian needed to be, I did not mean by that that he or she should be in a seminary rather than in a university. I was speaking, not about his location, but about his basic orientation and commitment. And now I want to insist on the complementary truth that that basic commitment does not exonerate him from the need to submit the beliefs and teachings of the church to every appropriate test with the same measure of intellectual rigour that his secular colleagues (if he has such) would use in the pursuit of their studies. His context within the church does not provide any source of authority that is exempt from critical scrutiny of that kind. And it is only the theologian who is prepared to add to his commitment to the tradition a commitment to that kind of critical scrutiny who deserves to be attended to.

But how is so hazardous an enterprise to be carried through? No fixed criteria for testing the acceptability of theological proposals can be laid down in advance. For the kind of changes that are called for in the work of theology do not consist of moves to right or left along a line, so that the bounds of admissibility can be spelt out in advance. Like many changes in scientific or historical understanding they involve paradigm shifts of a subtle and all-encompassing kind. A much-used example of such a paradigm shift is the change from seeing the earth as the centre of the universe to seeing the earth as a satellite of the sun, which is itself the centre only of our solar system – one among countless others. That process involved not just new knowledge but coming to see all the evidence from a new perspective. Theological changes are often of that kind. Indeed, theology has had to go through many such shifts in the course of its history – from its earliest days as it came to terms with the fact that the coming of Christ was not the immediate prelude to the winding up of God's purposes in human history, through the disruption of the religious assumptions of mediaeval Europe at the Reformation and then the disruption of its cultural assumptions at the Enlightenment – on to the many changes of our own time, such as (to name but one) the changing attitude towards other religious faiths. To try to test new theological proposals that arise out of wrestling with changes of that sort by the application of theological formulas from the past is like trying to judge the acceptability of impressionism by the canons of classical art. Neither the form nor the extent that such critical reappraisal may appropriately take can be measured in that sort of way. There are no such short cuts in the process of assessment. New theological proposals involving a change of perspective of that kind can only be properly evaluated over a period of time. For it takes time to tell how effectively any such proposal enables one to do justice to the evidence from the past, how successfully it illuminates the present, and what promise it may hold out for the future in terms both of theory and practice.

3. And that is why the third feature of the profile that I am outlining of the true theologian is as vital as the other two. However firmly he or she be rooted in the tradition, however careful and serious the wrestling with that tradition in the light of the present, those facts do not authorize the theologian to put forward the outcome of his or her work as something that ought to find immediate acceptance in the church. The process is too subjective for that. Such subjectivity is not a fault; it is inescapable. All theology that is worth attending to has and must have something of the character of a personal vision. But this unavoidably subjective and personal character of all theological

work means that, however well done, it always runs the risk of distortion. In a similar way the moralist and the art-critic cannot get at the truths of their disciplines apart from their own experience and their own evaluation of the issues involved, and for that very reason need to submit their insights and their theories to the inter-subjective testing of others; so too the theologian. Richard Niebuhr put the point forcefully. Referring to the witness of the Christian tradition, past and present, he wrote: 'Without direct confrontation there is no truth for me in all such testimony; but without companions, collaborators, teachers, corroborating witnesses, I am at the mercy of my imagination.'[6] So just as the true theologian's work grows out of commitment to the Christian community, it must also be offered back to that community – to be tried out in the thinking, the living and the worshipping of the community as a whole.

Karl Rahner, who has done as much work as any recent theologian on this interface between the teachings of the tradition and the challenge of the modern world, expresses his confidence that whatever the tensions to which this process may give rise, it will never lead to insoluble conflict between the theologian and the church. 'A Catholic Christian', he writes, 'regards it as an impossible dilemma that he would have to choose between losing the truth of Christ and such a radical disobedience to the authority of the church that the concrete authority of the church would be denied or rejected.'[7] But Rahner is only able to say that because he has just spoken of a teaching authority in the church which, because it is sent by Christ and speaks in the name of Christ, can proclaim a teaching which is binding. And it is just such a conception of the teaching office of the church that I have already expressed myself unable to accept – for all the weight that I believe must be put on the need to drink deep from the wisdom of the tradition. But I agree with Rahner to this degree. A theologian must indeed be very slow to accept that such an irresolvable confrontation has been reached. If the vision that one offers as one's vision of the truth fails to find acceptance, it is only after further time and further self-critical reflection that one should reaffirm it with the kind of definiteness that Rahner describes. One should not come easily or quickly to the point where one says over against the church, 'Here I stand: I can do no other.' But the possibility that that moment may come cannot be ruled out.

It may seem that all I have done so far is to argue myself, and my so-called authentic theologian, into a position where we are more likely to be a source of disruption than of strength in the life of the church. Certainly the approach that I have been advocating stresses not only the inevitability but also the potential benefit of theological difference and disagreement. There are two reasons for that. The first I illustrated by my quotation from John McManners. There is no way of getting things right in a changing world that can avoid sometimes getting them wrong (at times quite seriously wrong) on the way. When the church had to come to terms, for example, with the critical study of the Bible, its doctrine of scripture could not remain unchanged. What changes were appropriate could only be discovered by a process of trial and error – indeed, that sentence should be in the present tense because we are still a part of that unfinished process. The second reason for a pluralism in theology is a more positive one that I have also been stressing in this lecture, namely the element of personal vision that is integral to any valid theology. But the personalism I have been trying to describe is a far cry from individualism. It recognizes that the personal vision essential to the work of theology has to arise out of and be offered back to the wider community. It is not therefore in conflict with concern for the unity of the church. What it does involve is a particular understanding of how we need to proceed if we are to secure that that unity will also be a unity in the truth.

As an example of the positive potential of this way of seeing the theologian's role in the church, let me take one feature of the contemporary ecumenical situation. When today we look back to the past, to the time of the Reformation or to other occasions in history which have given rise to the present divisions between Christians, we no longer feel the need to say that the fault lay all on one side. The best spokesmen on each side all had important insights into the nature of faith. And where they broke apart, each has gone on to build up a valid (if one-sided) form of Christian life and thought, centered upon the particular insight dominant in its own tradition at that time. It is important for the churches today to develop a sympathetic interpretation of each other's pasts; and there the historical theologian can assist us. But we do not need then to go back and rework the old ground in a new, more uniform way. Or rather, we cannot do so. There is no such going back and rewriting our history. The value of reviewing the old history is so that we can listen with more understanding to the insights and affirmations of our ecumenical partner *now*. All true theology, I have argued, is a wrestling with the tradition we have received in the light of the changing pattern of contemporary consciousness. And for the genuinely ecumenical theologian one feature of that contemporary consciousness is the different forms of Christian understanding to be found in Christian traditions other than one's own. So the theology that the ecumenical situation calls for is not some single, unified, systematic theology, as some official ecumenical conversations seem to assume. It calls rather for forms of catholic theology and forms of protestant theology which come out of their own traditions, but which, in the process of reworking those traditions, a process that is, I have been arguing, at the heart of all theological construction, have listened to and learnt from one another.

This account of how the theologian can contribute to the life of the church, both ecumenically and within his or her own confession, is not very widely accepted. That it can be disturbing and disconcerting is beyond dispute. But that is also a character-istic of the gospel itself. And, as I have been arguing, there is no other way in which the theologian can work which is consistent with the church's commitment to the search for truth. Moreover, it is disturbing and disconcerting primarily where stress is laid on tidiness and good order. Whereas it is my claim that the picture I have been describing is not only inescapable if our concern is with the search for truth, but that it also actually coheres better with the experience of living out the faith. For to live out our faith (in whatever way we understand that faith to come to us) involves the continual struggle to relate the tradition we have received to the changing realities of our time. And that is precisely what the theologian is doing. So the theologian, as I said at the outset, is only doing in a more concentrated way something in which we are all engaged. His work, therefore, should not be seen as marginal or abstruse (as is implied by the pejorative use of the word 'theological' so widely used by the press) but as directly related to the experience of every reflective Christian.

But if this understanding of the theologian's task is not widely accepted, it seems to me to be vital to the well-being of the church that it should come to be. What is required is a spirit of trust towards the theologian on the part of the church at large, born of a better appreciation of the theologian's task, and a spirit of humility on the part of the theologian, born of a recognition of the limited perspective from which he or she writes and speaks. Recent controversy in the Church of England shows little sign of the presence of the former. Whether the latter is any more in evidence is not for me to say. Moses may appear at times in the tradition as a dominating (even domineering) and authoritative figure – hardly the most obvious model for the spirit which I am looking for in the church of our own day. Yet to recall the incident with which I began, we could, I believe, all profit from the spirit of generosity and openness with which he was ready to acknowledge that the Lord might be speaking through even the irregular and unexpected voices of an Eldad or a Medad, prophesying outside the camp.

8

The Reasonableness of Christianity

For the last fourteen years, I have had the good fortune to share with Basil Mitchell in the conduct of a series of seminars on the relationship between philosophy and theology.[1] I have learned a great deal from them, but some fundamental puzzles still remain. It seems appropriate therefore in this context to try to articulate what is for me the basic perplexity about how work in philosophy of religion and theology ought to proceed.

My title expresses an aspiration which I believe the philosopher of religion and the theologian ought to hold in common. It is not, of course, original. I did not choose it in order to talk about Locke. But having chosen it, I find that he does in fact provide a possible starting-point. Locke's path to producing a reasonable Christianity was by way of what he calls 'an attentive and unbiased search' of scripture. Reliance on such a procedure was rendered reasonable by the evidence of prophecy and miracle. Its outcome was the delineation of a set of propositions which God had made a necessary part of the law of faith, and which it is our duty to embrace with docility as truths coming from God. Such a form of revelation, Locke suggests, fits the all-merciful God's concern for men whose hands are used to the plough and spade (to say nothing of the other sex).[2] I call this a possible starting-point only in the sense that it provides a vivid reminder of how different an approach is required of us, with our very different understanding of scripture, if we in our day are to be able to speak of the reasonableness of Christianity.

Before we consider whether we are in a position to speak in such terms, we need to consider what such a phrase might mean. Two distinctions are worth making at the outset. By 'the reasonableness of Christianity' we might mean either (a) that there are good reasons for being a Christian or (b) that reason is a vital constituent in determining the content of Christian belief. There is no necessary logical connection between those two. It would be possible to claim that there were good reasons (perhaps of a Pascalian wager kind) for assenting to Christianity even though the content of the faith might be determined in some wholly non-rational manner. Alternatively the content of the faith might be determined in a wholly rational manner, like an algebraic system, while there were no good grounds for believing that it related to any reality, this-worldly or other-worldly.

My second distinction is between (a) the claim that there are good reasons for being a Christian and that it is important that there are such reasons and (b) the claim that reason does in fact play a major role in determining whether or not people become Christians. The second may well be false, as I suspect it is; but the first might still be true. Psychological or sociological factors may play a predominant role in determining why particular people become Christian – the accident of birth, some favourable early association with Christianity, or some particular mystical or conversion experience. Reason at that point may not have had any significant role to play. But it may still be important for such people to be able to see their Christian position as reasonable, if they are to stay Christian. Much discussion of the reasonableness of Christianity is *post-factum* rationalization of that kind. Its occurring in that way does not render it valueless.

Historically the attitude of Christians to reason has been varied in the extreme. At one end of the spectrum we have the insistence that Athens has nothing to do with Jerusalem, that reason, and faith relate to totally different dimensions of experience, that reason is the devil's whore and has no standing-ground in relation to Christian truth. At the other we have the claim that the existence of God can be demonstrated by a process of deductive reasoning and that the absolute reliability of scripture can be convincingly proved by the testimony of miracle and fulfilled prophecy. Extreme claims of either kind are in my judgment wholly implausible. Claims of the first kind allow no room for discriminating between equally clamant claims of competing sects to be embodiments of the one true self-authenticating faith.

Claims of the latter kind have proved quite unable to stand up to the challenges that philosophical critics have levelled against them. I shall not waste time by going over the arguments once again. I recall those extreme positions only as providing the context within which the serious and difficult problems begin.

But even if we can ignore the largely non-existent 'pure fideists' and 'pure rationalists' we are faced with the immensely difficult task of mapping out an appropriate course through the extensive terrain that lies between those two extremes. To be 'reasonable' is a much broader concept than to be a follower of a set of specifiable rules of logic. The first thing about which we have to be absolutely clear and firm is that we do not have to choose between being 'rational' on the one hand (after the model of the pure mathematician with his wholly deductive proofs) and being 'irrational' on the other (in the sense of being unamenable to reasoning of any kind). As Stephen Toulmin among others has insisted, the form of reasoning appropriate in any particular discipline depends on the nature of that discipline and cannot be taken over without modification from what has proved itself appropriate in some other discipline.[3] Thus the theologian who aspires to be reasonable has no already existing pattern of reasonableness simply waiting to be picked up and applied. He or she has to find the appropriate method and the appropriate norms *in via*. All theologians worthy of the name are in fact engaged in a process of this kind. But it is a difficult and perplexing task. The basic perplexity, to which I referred at the start of this paper, can be very broadly stated in terms of the spatial metaphor used at the beginning of this paragraph. Most philosophers of religion, who ought to be helping the theologians in their mapping exercise, seem to me to keep too close for comfort to either the fideistic or the rationalistic bank – or, perhaps I should say, seem to keep for comfort too close to one of the two banks. The theologian, I believe, needs to travel a more difficult route somewhere nearer to the middle of the stream, and without more help from the philosopher of religion than is actually forthcoming the theologian is hard pressed to steer a proper course. I will try to illustrate what I mean with some more specific examples.

I begin with those who cling to the fideistic bank. The name of Wittgenstein has given a new philosophical status to the fideistic approach to Christianity in recent decades. 'Wittgensteinian fideism' sounds a lot more respectable than fideism *tout simple*. How faithful the various brands of it to be found in the contemporary academic market are to Wittgenstein himself is something I am not competent to assess; nor is it directly germane to my argument. Let me simply give two examples from the American scene of the kind of approach I have in mind. Both explicitly argue that the theism/atheism debate, which is normally conceived of as the basic issue in establishing a 'reasonable Christianity', is misconceived, and that no such debate can reasonably be carried on.

The first is Paul van Buren, probably still best known in England for his *Secular Meaning of the Gospel*, which was based on a strongly positivist account of language. But his later book, *The Edges of Language*, represents a sharp reaction away from his earlier views. In it he makes his main point with the aid of the same kind of topographical analogy that I have been using. 'God' for him is 'a word marking the outer edge of language', and if it is not 'then it falls within our clear, regular use of words and must stand the tests of coherence which rule what I should call the great central plains of our talk'. Here full attention is certainly given to the mysteriousness or (in Ian Ramsey's phrase) the logical oddity of our God talk. But this appears to be done in a crudely dichotomous way. On the one hand is a 'clear, regular use of words' with established tests of coherence; on the other hand are the edges of language where 'the categories of coherence . . . simply do not apply'.[4] This sharp dichotomy runs right through the book. Religious language is either language at the limit of its use or it is assertions;[5] the word 'God' is either a border-marker, a cry as we stumble at the edge of utter nonsense, or it is being understood literalistically.[6] By lumping together every position other than his own as a form of literalism van Buren can make traditional theology appear utterly implausible; but only at the cost of rendering his own wanderings around the edges of language vacuous. Christians do more than simply cry 'God'; they cry 'God' in a sophisticated variety of ways. Van Buren does not help us determine which of those ways are appropriate and why.

My second example is Paul Holmer's book *The Grammar of Faith*. Again the title of the book is significant. Having rightly emphasized the complexity of religious language and the need to take account of the ways and contexts within which it is used, Holmer goes on to speak of doctrines as 'the rules and grammar of the language of faith'.[7] Certainly there are analogies between the way doctrines function in the church and the way conventions of speech and behaviour function in other social groups. But let that analogy dominate one's understanding of Christian belief, and the concept of the truth or reasonableness of Christianity is ruled out absolutely in a way that seems to be wholly unacceptable.

To pick up again my analogy of the stream, such writers (if they have actually left the fideistic bank at all) seem to me to be moving about in the shallows under its lee. I do not think the Christian believer or the Christian theologian should follow their siren voices.

So, as my original choice of title has already clearly indicated, I am more attracted to those who stress the role of reason in relation to belief. But reason, as we have already seen, takes different forms in different contexts. Careful attention needs, therefore, to be given to the way in which reason is understood to function. The two examples that I shall take in this case are two English scholars, Richard Swinburne and Anthony Kenny, one a Christian believer and the other not, who have both published books entitled *Faith and Reason* in the early 1980s.[8]

Swinburne closes the introduction to his earlier book *The Coherence of Theism* with these words:

It is one of the intellectual tragedies of our age that when philosophy in English-speaking countries has developed high standards of argument and clear thinking, the style of theological writing has been largely influenced by the continental philosophy of Existentialism, which, despite its considerable other merits, has been distinguished by a very loose and sloppy style of argument. If argument has a place in theology, large-scale theology needs clear and rigorous argument. That point was very well grasped by Thomas Aquinas and Duns Scotus, by Berkeley, Butler, and Paley. It is high time for theology to return to their standards.[9]

That is a noble ideal. But how is it to be put into practice? The primary strategy of both writers is to emphasize the extent to which language about God can be understood in a straightforward, non-analogical sense. This has obvious advantages for the application of rational argument to issues of theistic belief, for, as Swinburne puts it, where words are used analogically the syntactic and semantic rules that govern their use have to be modified with the result that 'the less clear it will be what is being said'.[10]

The point is an important one and it is worth looking in a little more detail at how it works out in their writings. Anthony Kenny's book *The God of the Philosophers* is a careful consideration of the two traditional divine attributes, omniscience and omnipotence. At the start of the book he gives his reasons for concentrating on those two particular attributes.

> Other attributes, such as justice, mercy, and love have a more obvious significance for the religious believer; but they are less immediately amenable to philosophical investigation and analysis ... Whatever significance these predicates ['just', 'merciful' and 'loving'] have when applied to God, they cannot be understood simply in the same sense as when applied to human beings. Intellect and power, on the other hand, are intended to be attributed to God in the most literal sense: it is the infinity of the intellect and the limitlessness of the power that makes the difference between the creator and the creature. 'Omniscient' and 'omnipotent' are not predicates which were in use for application to human beings and are then ascribed in some transferred or analogical sense to God: they express concepts which were devised to represent uniquely divine characteristics.[11]

But is Kenny's argument sound? It may well be true that moral and personal attributes, like justice, mercy, and love, are less

immediately amenable to philosophical analysis than intellect
and power. But it does not follow from that fact that the two sets
of attributes apply to God in different ways. Nor is the
etymological fact that 'omniscient' and 'omnipotent' are words
applied directly to God of any significance. The OED provides us
with 'all-just' and 'all-merciful', of which the same could be
said.[12] I see no ground for acknowledging (as Kenny appears to
do) the analogical attribution of justice, mercy, and love to God,
but not of intellect and power. If that is right, it is of great
importance for the assessment of Kenny's argument. For the
conclusion to which he is led at the end of his discussion is 'that
there cannot . . . be a timeless, immutable, omniscient,
omnipotent, all-good being'.[13] But unless Kenny was justified in
denying the analogical character of the attribution of intellect and
power to God, his argument can be challenged for failing to allow
for those modifications of syntactic and semantic rules that
govern the use of analogical terms.

Swinburne pursues a very similar line of argument in *The
Coherence of Theism*. He too discusses the intelligibility of the
divine attributes, omnipotence and omniscience, without ap-
pealing to any analogical usage of the terms 'power' or 'knowledge'. He only 'plays the analogical card', as he puts it, very late
on in the book, when he comes to speak of God as personal.[14]
Since the conclusion to which he comes is 'that it is coherent to
suppose that there exists eternally an omnipresent spirit, perfectly
free, the creator of the universe, omnipotent, omniscient,
perfectly good, and a source of moral obligation',[15] his argument
is not open to the same objections as Kenny's. For if the argument
holds when the terms are understood in a literal sense, *a fortiori* it
will be impossible to dismiss as incoherent any modified analogical (and therefore less precise) interpretation which the
theologian may rightly want to give to such an account of God
(whatever other objections his analogical interpretation may be
open to).

There is neither scope here, nor have I the philosophical
competence, to judge between the substance of their two
arguments. I want rather to raise the question of whether their
style of reasoning is the most appropriate for a philosopher of

religion to adopt. That would clearly be a crucial question for any Christian philosopher of religion who was not convinced that Swinburne's argument held. But quite apart from the outcome of any assessment of the actual conduct of the argument, there are reasons for questioning whether it does represent the form of argument appropriate to the nature of God, as Christians have understood it. In a generally appreciative review of Kenny's *Faith and Reason* Keith Ward argues that he ought to have devoted more attention to the fact 'that God has generally been regarded by classical Christian theologians as a unique kind of being, not just another member of a class of finite objects'.[16] Criticism along those lines seems to me to have force, though it clearly requires careful and detailed substantiation. For our present purpose I want to pursue the implications of the approach followed by Kenny and Swinburne, not so much for the philosopher of religion as for the theologian.

The metaphor with which Swinburne chooses to speak about the impact of analogy on reasoned argument is that of a card game. The appeal to analogy is 'a joker which it would be self-defeating to play more than two or three times in a game'.[17] As we have already seen, he believes the card does need to be played in speaking of God as personal. But the theologian has to speak of God as personal in very concrete ways most of the time. He speaks of a God who loves and saves, who becomes incarnate and makes atonement for human sins. Can he then do so in a way that is amenable to reason? One cannot have a game in which every card is a joker. The theologian is looking for a style of reasoning which can operate with a language about God in which the presence of analogy is not an occasional phenomenon but a fundamental characteristic. The way in which Kenny and Swinburne stress the conflict between analogical usage and reasoned argument does not encourage the theologian in that search. Yet Swinburne exhorts the theologian, and not merely the philosopher of religion, to adopt the way of 'clear and rigorous argument'. How then does he expect the theologian to follow his counsel?

Swinburne's answer emerges most clearly when he turns to more doctrinal concerns in the later sections of his *Faith and Reason*. The more specifically doctrinal work of Christian theology needs a quite different base. It needs 'God's announcement to man of things beyond his power to discover for himself',[18] which can be known to be 'true without qualification' or simply 'because of the prophet's authority'.[19] And for that authority to be known to be God's there must be 'some kind of miraculous signature symbolically affirming and forwarding the prophet's teaching and work'.[20] Paley is adjudged to have been right when he wrote: 'In what way can a revelation be made, but by miracles? In none which we are able to conceive.'[21] The understanding of faith which Kenny chooses to discuss in his *Faith and Reason* is remarkably similar. It is the belief in certain truths not ascertainable by human reason which God has revealed about himself to the human race.[22] His reason for concentrating attention on that understanding of faith is that 'it is the one which was most explicitly articulated to safeguard the concerns of reason'.[23] But since he declares himself to 'have rejected the classical definition of rationality',[24] ought he not also to be ready to abandon this classical conception of faith?

In my initial reference to Locke I spoke of his book as 'a vivid reminder of how different an approach is required of us'. Yet Swinburne in particular (for all his acknowledgment of the difference in detail required by advances in historical knowledge) seems to have led us back to something very like Locke's starting-point. But in leading us back there, he has not shaken my conviction that it is no longer a possible starting-point for us today. I do not see how any theologian who has given serious attention to the work done by biblical scholars could begin to pursue the work of Christian theology in the way that Swinburne proposes. Initial misgivings about the appropriateness of the style of reasoning in his own field of the philosophy of religion are reinforced by the conception of faith that appears to be its natural concomitant.

So my perplexity remains. One of the things which as a theologian I hope to gain from philosophers of religion is some guidance as to the appropriate form that reasoning should take in the work of theology. Yet the writings of many of the ablest and most distinguished scholars in that field do not seem to have much help to offer. Nevertheless, I still retain the conviction that there is a route to be found somewhere nearer to the middle of the stream, which combines a full recognition of the indirectness and logical oddity of our religious language with an equally strong insistence on the referential character and the truth claims of Christian discourse and also on the need for appropriate modes of reasoning about those claims. So it is incumbent on me to say something about how I think that path might be followed, even though it was my dissatisfaction with anything I found myself able to say on the subject that prompted my writing this paper in the first instance.

I am convinced that we do need to test our religious utterances for coherence and credibility, if we are not simply to be swept giddily on with van Buren along, or over, the edges of language. There is enough religious mystification and double-talk around for this to be a vital task. But I am equally convinced that because of the indirectness of our religious affirmations the task cannot be done as straightforwardly as some other writers suggest. How we are to proceed will depend on how we think our language about God arises. This is a vast and controversial topic in its own right, and all I can do in this context is to spell out briefly my own understanding of the matter and its implications for our present topic. Fundamentally I believe that our language about God is built up by a process of 'symbolization' or 'imaginative construction',[25] that it to say that we take certain fundamental aspects of our human experience and extend them to their limits, in the conviction that that process will provide us with the least inadequate pointers to the nature of that ultimate reality, which is the source and goal of our existence. Thus the fact that we are dependent, not self-created, beings; that we are limited by death; that our knowledge is limited yet always capable of further developments; that we sense ourselves to be challenged to goodness and obligation from beyond ourselves – these things give rise to our speaking of God as creator, as immortal, as omniscient, as perfect. Reflection on this process may convince us that such a way of speaking is rationally defensible, while still leaving open the question of in what precise manner the language is to be understood. But for the Christian believer language about God does not arise simply in this abstract form. In Christian discourse it takes on a much more specific form on the basis of particular historical moments in the prophetic tradition of Israel, culminating in the coming of Jesus, at which such experiences have arisen in especially transparent and transformative ways. In particular such language has taken the form of stories concerning God's revelation in Christ – incarnational, adoptionist, etc. – and stories relating to atonement – a cosmic struggle with the powers of evil, meeting the demands of an immutable law, etc.

Of course, for us this language comes embodied in a well-established tradition. I am certainly not suggesting that each of us individually has consciously built up our forms of Christian speech in this way. But our traditional forms of Christian speech, though well-established, are not uniform or fixed. They come to us in diverse and fluctuating ways. And that is one important reason why it is not enough to regard doctrines as simply the rules of the grammer of faith. There is not just one homogeneous language of the Christian tradition. My reflection on the basic roots of such language was designed to help our consideration of how we ought to go about trying to sort out apparent confusion or conflict within the tradition which we have inherited. To ask what form of the tradition is most coherent is one important test, but it is not enough. Such a purely formal approach is in danger of losing contact with the root sources of our puzzling religious affirmations. So we need also from time to time to trace the language back to its experiential base, and ask again whether we have drawn upon that experience rightly and appropriately in our developed application of it to God. Something like this is recommended by Keith Ward in his book *The Concept of God*, which combines a concern with the ways in which faith in God has actually arisen and does arise together with a concern about the philosophical analysis of the concept of God, in a manner which is rarer than it ought to be in theological writing. He says:

It may be that the concepts which derive from diverse types of experience do not fall together to form one systematic and coherent whole. It may be even they seem contradictory – as with talk of Divine immutability and compassion for human suffering. But if one can show how one comes to talk of God in

these ways for different purposes, the difficulties are mitigated.[26]

'Mitigated' is, I think, the right word; the difficulties certainly do
not disappear. We ought not to glory in the paradox. We should
go on seeking greater coherence in our language and understanding, but not at the cost of riding roughshod over some well-
attested aspect of the experiences of the Christian community.
We should always regard such paradoxes as provisional, even
though they may in fact turn out to be permanent.

But what of the more elaborate story form of developed
doctrines of christology or atonement? Can a similar strategy
help us to decide between competing accounts? It would be nice if
we could appeal in a more or less direct way to what we
sometimes call the 'logic' of the story. But as the gospel parables
remind us, though the stories which we are led to tell about God
may have their own logic, it is often very different from the logic
of prior human expectation. In practice I think that we need to
proceed in a way very similar to that which I am proposing for
assessing the appropriateness of ascribing particular attributes to
God. Despite the difference in the style of affirmation, the
underlying issues in, for example, a consideration of the appropriateness of telling the atonement story in terms of God
meeting the demands of a law of his own devising are very similar
to those involved in the process alluded to by Ward of trying to
determine the compatability of ascribing to God both compassion and immutability. Although such stories can never be
simply replaced by an equivalent conceptual statement without
loss, some approximate translation into conceptual terms is
always possible. And both the story and the conceptual terms
have roots in our human experience.

So I have no clear-cut recipe to offer of how we may give a
reasonable account of faith in God and of Christian belief. Any
claim of being able to offer an account of such a kind ought in any
case always to be received with sceptical suspicion. As with moral
reasoning, what is needed is not a clear process for settling all
disputed issues – that is a will o' the wisp – but rather a recognized
process of reasoning, even though many substantial differences of

judgment may still remain unresolved in the process of applying it.[27] What I have tried to stress is the need for a continuous to and fro movement between the experiential and metaphorical roots of faith and its more direct expression in religious practice and worship on the one hand, and careful and critical reflection at the conceptual level on the other.[28] Neither the precise form of these two activities nor the exact balance between them can be spelled out in advance. Like most comparable skills it is an art that can be learned only by the doing of it. My impression, as this paper has indicated, is that many of our ablest writers attach themselves too exclusively to the one pole or the other. My conviction is that there is a navigable course in the middle of the stream, and my plea is that the imaginative and critical skills of all concerned with the study of religions should be appropriately conjoined in the never-ending search for it.

9

Worship and Theology

The office of canon-professor combines responsibility for the regular ordering of cathedral worship with responsibility for the pursuit of critical scholarship within a university. It is a combination that cannot always be practised without tension. Can one pursue at one and the same time the kind of commitment inherent in Christian worship and the kind of critical study inherent in the work of theology within a university context, when that study is directly focussed on that to which one is committed in one's worship? It was my privilege to share this sometimes awkward dual responsibility in Oxford for many years with Peter Baelz. Through his teaching, his example and above all his friendship during those years he taught me a great deal about how the two parts of the job could fruitfully be held together. This essay seeks to draw upon that inspiration and offer some reflections on the relationship between worship and critical theology.

'He who comes to God must first believe that he is and that he is a rewarder of those who seek him.' So the Epistle to the Hebrews (11.6), and it seems a reasonable enough proposition. Worship is a form of coming to God, of coming 'before his presence with thanksgiving', as the Venite calls on us to do in the invitation to worship at the start of Anglican Matins. That, it may well be claimed, logically requires a prior 'faith in the existence and in the moral government of God' (to use Bishop Westcott's paraphrase of the Hebrews text).[1] But what is the nature of that prior faith? Peter Baelz spoke at length in his Bampton lectures, *The Forgotten Dream*, about the 'half-believer'.[2] The half-believer, as he rightly insists, is a totally different species from the half-hearted believer. The question of belief is one of passionate concern to the half-believer. But he is one for whom the evidence, both intellectual and experiential, will not fall into a pattern that constitutes a settled conviction. There is no way in which he or she can first establish a firm belief in the existence of God and in his moral government of the world and then come to God in worship. Nor is his or her half-belief the kind of thing that is open to a probabilistic calculus, which exceeds 50% one week allowing one to join in worship, but falls to 49% the next forcing one conscientiously to abstain. Faith in God is not like that. The dual format of the Hebrews text can, indeed, easily be misleading. There are not two separate questions. Does God exist? and Are his dealings with us and with the world moral? – as if one could answer the first with certainty while still being in doubt about the second. The problematic character of the meaning of the word 'God', as somehow the ground both of existence and goodness, is part of what puzzles the half-believer. And the half-believer's intellectual studies will certainly continue to feed his or her doubts and sense of puzzlement. But few of us, I suspect, would want to exclude such a person from the practice of Christian worship. If there are difficulties about the half-believer's participation, they should more properly arise from the conscientious hesitation of the half-believer him or herself than from exclusivist zeal on the part of church authorities.

Anthony Kenny in the moving close to his book, *The God of the Philosophers*, has pushed similar reflections a stage further. His book displays a more clearly defined understanding of the word 'God' and a more decided agnosticism about his existence, yet one which falls a long way short of convinced atheism; but the book also gives voice to the same insistence on the fundamental importance of the question. In its final pages Kenny argues for the reasonableness of prayer on the part of one such as himself for guidance and illumination from the God who may possibly exist.[3] If such prayer can seem reasonable to the agnostic himself, it should do so even more to any Christian for whom the kind of experience of God claimed to be characteristic of prayer and worship is seen as a fundamental feature of the grounding of belief in God.

In recalling the work of Peter Baelz and Anthony Kenny I have been arguing that the half-believer and the agnostic may wish to participate in Christian worship, and that such a wish should be welcomed by the Christian community. In first century Corinth unbelievers (for whatever motives) seem sometimes to have attended the church's worship, and in his first letter to the Corinthians Paul even suggests that, if they are not attracted by what they hear, the fault may not necessarily lie with them but may lie rather with the form of worship adopted (I Cor. 14.23–5). But such an attitude was short-lived. In the case of unbelievers, precaution against possible informers will have played a part. But more theoretical justifications soon played their part too, if indeed they were not part of the story from the outset. Such theoretical justifications were not exclusively Christian in origin. An esoteric attitude was part of the surrounding religious ethos, clearly exemplified in the mystery religions. But soon more explicitly theological reasons became the dominant force. Not only outsiders but fellow-Christians with divergent forms of Christian belief were not to be accepted as fellow worshippers. That attitude is still very much with us. It is wrong, we are often told, a form of dishonesty indeed, to share in eucharistic worship with those who have a different understanding of what is happening in the sacramental service. The Catholic Ecumenical Directory, for example, still requires each individual member of any other Western Christian body, who is without access to eucharistic ministry in his or her own communion, to demonstrate that he or she has a faith in the eucharist in conformity with that of the Catholic Church before such a person can share in Catholic eucharistic worship.[4] Of course there are many issues involved in such a judgment. But set it in the context of what I have just been saying about the participation of the half-believer and the agnostic in Christian worship, and it is hard not to conclude that concern for institutional control over the community may be a more powerful factor in the case than the impropriety of people with different understandings sharing in a common act of worship.

It is interesting to observe the gradual emergence of this exclusivist attitude to Christian worship, and its application to those judged to be deviants in the matter of belief. The Fourth Gospel tells us that the worship of God must be 'in spirit and truth' (John 4.24). The earliest Christian exegesis of that text gives a broad interpretation to the word 'truth'. Our worship must pass beyond the level of type and shadow; it must be at the level of the ultimate, the real. As the true light and the true vine belong not to the realm of the senses but to the suprasensible realm, so the same contrast underlies the insistence that worship must be worship in the truth. But by the end of the fourth century a marked change of emphasis has emerged. The earlier interpretation is not completely forgotten. But the main stress has changed. Worship in the truth is, above all, worship in conformity with the dogmatic teaching of the church.[5]

Exegesis of another verse from that same context of Jesus' discourse with the Samaritan woman figures prominently in one of those fourth century debates in a way that bears directly on the issue with which I am concerned. Just before the injunction to worship God in spirit and in truth, Jesus is described as saying to the Samaritan woman 'you worship what you do not know; we worship what we know' (John 4.22). Eunomius, the fourth century Neo-Arian, made much of it in his controversy with the Cappadocian Fathers. That worship in truth was worship in accordance with the dogmatic teaching of the church was common ground between them. But Eunomius, employing a realist theory of language in which names depict the essence of what is named, presses the point home with rigour. Christian revelation communicates the true name of God. When Moses asked God his name, the answer came back: 'I am that I am. Tell them that I am has sent you to them' (Ex. 3.14). God is the great I Am, ὁ ὤν underived being, Being itself. Christians have been enabled to know the very essence of God. True worship is worship of what we know. Any worship that is equivocal about our knowledge of God's essence is not Christian worship. It is Samaritan worship of what one does not know; it is pagan Athenian worship of an unknown God.[6]

His Cappadocian opponents did not deny that revelation tells us many things about God: about his trinitarian nature and about his attributes. But Eunomius' claim to know the essence of God amounted in their eyes to the ultimate blasphemy of claiming to know as much about God as God himself knows. The highest knowledge of God open to us does not have that kind of clarity. It is to advance with Moses into the dark cloud on Mount Sinai, into the thick darkness which God is (Ex. 20.21); it is to grow in the recognition of our ignorance of what God in himself is, of what it is to be God. Moreover the knowledge about God that is communicated to us is communicated through the indirect medium of finite, human words and concepts. It tells us something about what God does, nothing about what he is. Even the word for God (θεός) is derived from the word to see and indicates God's oversight of the world, not his essence. And even that it can do only imperfectly, because the concepts it uses have their primary location in our human speech.

In that debate the sympathies of all of us lie, I suspect, with the Cappadocians – the sympathies even of those with a special concern to see some righting of the wrongs so often done in the past to the heretics of the early church. For the Cappadocians worship and philosophical reflection on language are more closely integrated into a coherent religious outlook than is commonly to be found in many of their modern counterparts. The two do not appear to be in tension. Both point in the same direction, in the direction of an apophaticism which their work did much to further as an important strain in the subsequent history of Christian thought. They are held back from the more radical agnosticism towards which it might seem to lead by their conviction about the clear and specific content of what is given in Christian revelation.

The problems that face us are not altogether unlike those that they had to face. And there are those who would counsel a return to something like their way of reading scripture as a way out of our difficulties. 'There is . . . no good reason', says George Lindbeck, 'in the present intellectual situation for not once again utilizing this pre-modern way of reading scripture'.[7] It is true that there is much that is attractive in the reading of scripture as 'a Christ-centred and typologically unified whole with figural application to all reality'[8] (to cite Lindbeck's own summary description of the pre-modern reading of scripture), and much to be learned from the insights of exegetes of earlier centuries. But their situation was different from ours, and the answer to our problems is not to be found in an attempt to recover a lost age of innocence, masquerading as a form of post-modernity. We have to explore the interrelation of worship and critical reflection, especially the philosophy of language, as an issue that bears directly on the viability of our faith. And if we start to suffer from vertigo in the process, there is no scriptural safety-net.

I have already indicated that there is no way of starting from the end of philosophical reflection and thereby establishing the truth of Christian claims about the existence and nature of God in such a way as to satisfy ourselves once for all about the validity of Christian worship. The problematic character of any such procedure is well enough known, and I restrict myself to one example of the kind of difficulty involved.

One form of such argumentation for the existence of God, which has not only been important historically but which in my view continues to be important philosophically also, is the argument from contingency. But the argument is not really a narrowly intellectual form of reasoning based on the logical status of contingency as such; its real basis is a way of experiencing the fact of contingency, which is closely akin to the underlying attitude implicit in the activity of worship.[9] An orientation towards the validity of the way of worship is already present in the grounding of the philosophical argument. The latter cannot function, therefore, as a logically prior step towards the establishment of the validity of the former.

Nor can we start with the practice of worship and use it to confirm the truth of our particular theological beliefs. The *lex orandi* has often been claimed to establish some specific aspect of the *lex credendi*. But it is usually easy enough to demonstrate that the particular form of the *lex orandi* to which appeal is being made has itself been determined not just out of the experience of praying but as the outcome of some prior theological argumentation. The late fourth century appeal to the language of the Gloria in Christian worship as evidence in support of an orthodox trinitarian belief is a clear case in point. The precise form of the language appealed to was in fact a product of the earlier years of that century, consciously adopted on the basis of commitment to the theological belief in question.[10] There is no such thing as the pure experience of worship which is uninfluenced by some preexisting theological understanding of God and of his relation to the world.

Thus the two, worship and theological reflection, are not to be found in isolation from each other. Nevertheless they are not identical, and it is important to recognize their distinctness and to consider the ways in which they interact on each other. One can draw an analogy with the two commandments to love God and to love our neighbour. For certain purposes we may rightly want to insist that the two are really one commandment – and that to love God and hate one's neighbour is not to fulfil half one's duty; rather it is a logical impossibility, because it is through love of the neighbour that love of God finds its expression. But for other purposes it may be necessary to emphasize their distinct but interrelated character, and seek by concentration on one to enlarge and modify our understanding and practice of the other. It is an approach of that kind that is called for if we are to further our understanding of how our worship and our critical theological reflection may not merely coexist but mutually reinforce one another.

The most obvious difference between the two is in their contrasting styles of language. The characteristic language of worship is poetic with its rich interplay of symbols. The characteristic language of philosophy and theology is a punctilious prose with its careful selection and ordering of concepts. I spoke just now of the 'interplay' of symbols in worship. The word 'interplay' is appropriate. For there the symbols seem often to be at play with a child-like innocence, trailing clouds of glory as they come from the rich imagery of their past in the Bible and in Christian tradition. But the language of playfulness invites the riposte that worship is either a form of sheer projection, contributing nothing to true knowledge, or else at best an epiphenomenon, depending for whatever cognitive validity it may have on the knowledge established by the more serious, if more prosaic activities of the philosopher and the theologian.

The riposte is familiar enough; but it has also enough plausibility and sufficient barb of truth that we need frequently to recall and to refresh our reasons for not accepting it. In so far as the objection is based on the analogy with poetry, it is based on a

very superficial view of poetry. 'Poetic metaphor', to cite Frank
Burch Brown, 'alters and expands one's ever finite understanding
of oneself and of the realities within and by which one lives'.[11]
And if that is true of poetry, there seems to me no good ground for
denying a similar cognitive role to worship. Such a view is
sensitively argued by Dan Hardy and David Ford in their book
Jubilate. They describe the praise of God as 'a key to the ecology
in which right knowledge of God grows'; in the activity of praise
'not only is God known . . . but also God enhances our rational
powers'.[12] In the nature of the case there can, of course, be no
proof that it is so. The most we can expect to claim is that the style
of language that is characteristic of worship appears in other
contexts to be a way to knowledge. Imaginative language does
not depict only the purely imaginary. As Janet Soskice has argued
with such care, the parallel of its use in other areas of discourse
(not least in the natural sciences) gives the theist reasonable
grounds for regarding the talk of God which it enables 'as reality
depicting, while at the same time acknowledging its inadequacy
as description'.[13]

It follows from what I have been saying that the radical
contrast between the style of language characteristic of worship
and that characteristic of critical theology does not reflect a
radical contrast of function. For one aspect of our worship is a
search for the true knowledge of God, which is the ultimate goal
also of the work of the critical theologian. As in other disciplines
the reflective exploration of basic images can fulfil an important
heuristic role. Imaginative construction is a necessary path
towards true knowledge. But it is a form of projection; and even
though not for that reason doomed to futility, it is highly fallible.
It is therefore in continued need of checking and correction. It
extends our knowing through enabling us to see things differently; but we need to be sure that it is genuine sight and not
illusion to which we have been brought. It enhances our rational
powers; but we need to be able to distinguish between an
enhancement and a renunciation.

Thus the practice of worship does not simply tolerate the
separate coexistence of critical theology, like the two halves of the
Nestorian Christ or as in the practice of apartheid. It positively

requires it; it needs its interaction. As Frank Burch Brown puts it, 'the fullest possible understanding of Christian faith ... is inherently dialogical ... it moves back and forth between metaphoric and conceptual thinking'.[14] But the movement is not an easy one. Conceptual thought cannot fully encompass the creative implication of the significant metaphor. But it is needed to provide some curb on the other's chaotic fecundity. The fundamental Christian conviction about the transcendence and the unity of God involves on the one hand an acknowledgment of the inadequacy of all our language about him, but also an insistence on the ultimate coherence of the varied affirmations which we are led to make. It is that latter task to which the philosopher-theologian is committed. He or she must pursue it with rigour, but also with a clear recognition of the incompleteness of all conceptual systems, including his or her own.

I have been presenting the philosopher-theologian's distinctive role as the careful corrector of the fecund creativity of the worshipper-poet. And that I believe is a very important aspect of that role. But it claims perhaps both too much and too little. Too much, because it suggests that theology can sit in judgment on the way of worship with the right to pronounce where it is true and where it is in error. But in fact it cannot dispose in that way; it can only propose, because its findings too are fallible, as are those of the way of imaginative projection. Yet also too little, because it suggests that the theological task is a wholly secondary and derivative activity. But it too has a creative role. The process, as Burch Brown says, is inherently dialogical. It is not only the symbol that gives rise to thought; 'the thought, in turn, gives rise to the symbol'.[15] That side of the process can only be a slow and gradual one. But it has happened in the history of the church down the ages, and it is important that it should continue to happen. Its most significant form is not the incorporation of the theologian's formula into the language of the liturgy, but the evocation of symbols or ritual patterns that give expression to, and take further, insights arising from the process of the theologian's critical reflections.

So the way of worship and the way of critical theology belong closely together. It is a conviction with which Hardy and Ford strongly concur in their book to which I have already referred. But they enter a caveat that deserves to be heeded. 'Both the praising and the knowing of God', they write, 'tend to be disconnected from the rest of living and knowing. Just relating them together might only increase their isolation in a religious ghetto'.[16] Has the approach I have been advocating left itself open to that risk? Two factors, I hope, will guard against it. In the course of the essay I have laid stress on the parallels with other disciplines in relation both to the role of imagery and of conceptual thought. The way to theological knowing is not radically different from the ways to other forms of knowledge. Good theology cannot flourish in isolation from the rest of knowing. Secondly one important criterion to be used in the critical task of theological reflection on the possibilities adumbrated by the religious imagination is a pragmatic one. It is not only the logical coherence of the religious visions to which worship may give rise by which critical theology seeks to test them. Another important criterion is their implications for human life and action – a theme much stressed in various forms of contemporary theology such as political, liberation or feminist theology. So once again good theology cannot flourish in isolation from the rest of living. The danger to which Hardy and Ford draw our attention is real enough. But the resources to meet it are already inherent in the structures of theological reflection.

I began this essay by recalling the obligation on a canon-professor to integrate the activities of worship and critical theology. I have tried to reflect on how that can appropriately be done at the level of theory. It is more simply summed up in the command to love the Lord your God with all your mind. The love with which we are to love God is a realistic love, not the blind love of infatuation which denies the evidence of defect or weakness in the object of its love. The Christian does, of course, deny defect or weakness in the object of his or her love; but he or she does not deny defect and weakness in the evidence. We see through a glass darkly. There are defects and weaknesses, not only in ourselves but also in the glass, which obscure and distort what we see. The commitment for which worship calls is not commitment to the vision just as it has been described by those who have gone before us; it is commitment to the struggle to interpret and to live by the confused images that we are enabled to glimpse with the help of what our predecessors have seen. And that calls for a rigorously critical and questioning spirit in theology.

A theology of such a kind is a necessary part of the process whereby we seek to ensure that our worship will be worship in the truth. And it may involve a conflict between the two traditional interpretations of that phrase that I spoke of earlier – worship in accordance with the dogmatic teaching of the church and worship at the level of the ultimate, of the real. Part, indeed, of the aim of this essay has been to try to provide a context for the better understanding of such conflict when it does arise – and in one form or another it is surely an aspect of the experience of many people today. If my account is on the right lines, it may help make it more possible for us to reaffirm our commitment to our specific forms of worship with renewed conviction, while at the same time enabling us to be clear, when conflict does arise between the two senses of 'worship in the truth', where it is that our primary allegiance lies.

Part Four

Theology

10

Can Theology Still Be about God?

Believing in God, like believing the earth to be flat, was once a basic belief but is so no longer. That is not to say that both are equally clearly false; the belief that the world is round is now both a basic belief and one with decisive evidence in its support, but atheism is not. So it is rather to say that belief in God is not today a part of the commonly accepted stock of beliefs, taken for granted within the community. It is something for which we can be expected to give reasons if we want to draw upon it in contemporary conversation or discussion.

The so-called arguments for the existence of God flourished with particular vigour when belief in God was a strongly held, basic belief. That fact gave rise to their ambiguous character, on which philosophers of religion have loved to fasten. Are they really arguments for the existence of God, or are they more properly described as reflections from within faith on what is involved in believing in God? The answer would seem to be that they are both. They arise from within a context of faith; how could they not, if belief in God was at the time a genuinely basic belief? That fact affects their form and structure but does not necessarily invalidate their status as arguments altogether. With the erosion of belief in God as a basic belief, more weight came to be placed on such arguments; and it was more weight than they were able to sustain.

One strand – or, better, a family of very diverse strands – in contemporary philosophy of religion and theology has welcomed unreservedly the collapse of arguments for God's existence. On the philosophical side, antifoundationalists have argued that any such grounding of faith is inappropriate and unnecessary, because we can never get behind our basic postulates to some neutral ground from which their validity could be demonstrated. Basic axioms are something we have to choose rather than justify. Belief in God is as 'reasonable' an axiom as any other. We may come to recognize its rightness from inside; we cannot ground it in anything external to itself. To try to do so is a sign of philosophical confusion. On the theological side, it is argued (usually with more or less direct inspiration from Karl Barth) that any such attempted grounding of faith is religiously inappropriate to a true understanding of God. God is not an object for our investigation; God is a subject who makes Godself known in God's own way – specifically, in Jesus Christ. 'Theism' for these theologians is a boo-word, indicative of a religious insensitivity that is little better than atheism. The reality of God can only be known from within obedient response to God's chosen form of self-revelation. It is sacrilegious to try to ground belief in God any other way.

Before we dismiss these responses as leading to an arbitrary irrationalism – as I believe, in the end, we are right to do – it is important to recognize the elements of truth and the attractiveness inherent in them. It is true that there is no neutral starting point. Arguments concerning the existence of God for the most part arise from within an already existing, broadly based commitment to or rejection of belief in God, and the form an argument takes is ineluctably influenced by those prior commitments. Moreover, the attractiveness of positions of the kind I have sketched is not only the force of their philosophical and religious insights but also the acute difficulty involved in developing any other strategy for upholding belief in God in an age where it is no longer a basic belief. Those difficulties are unlikely to diminish. It is already being claimed that the incoming currents of postmodern thought show the essential rightness of Barth's theological approach in even sharper relief than was evident in his own time.[1] Is there any path to be followed that will not take the form of a forlorn attempt to prop up the apparently discredited lines of argument embodied in the old proofs for the existence of God? A central feature of Gordon Kaufman's theological agenda has been to look for a third way that involves neither an 'attempt to argue the existence of God on theoretical grounds,' on the one hand, nor 'moving in a purely fideistic direction and simply proclaiming our belief that God exists despite all difficulties inherent in the situation', on the other hand.[2]

I have acknowledged that the old arguments were unable to carry the strain required of them by the transition to the modern world and are still less likely to be able to do so in any emerging postmodern world. Perhaps, however, we should think of them as having buckled, rather than broken, under that increased strain. Not everyone has responded to their collapse in the way that I have described. For some the old arguments have continued to be of significance, but in a much revised form. The ontological argument, always unique in its fundamental conception, has had a correspondingly special place of its own in the recent history of philosophical discussion; but I do not propose to pursue that in this essay. The cosmological and teleological arguments have been seen by many as raising genuine questions about the existence and intelligibility of the physical universe that ought not be dismissed out of hand as pseudo-questions. Nevertheless, they are not generally seen as pointing to the existence of God in the clear-cut way that has often been claimed for them in the past. In Paul Tillich's phrase, they raise rather than answer the question of God.[3]

Furthermore, if one surveys the work of twentieth-century theologians who have felt the need of supplying some grounding for the belief in God that they seek to expound, one finds it is not to those arguments that they have primarily turned. Instead, they have sought to establish an anthropological basis for their fundamental belief in God. Some aspect of what it is to be a human being has supplied their need for a reasoned grounding for the affirmation of God. There is nothing new in the fact of such appeals. One need only recall the inward turn so characteristic of Augustine's thought. Nevertheless, the fundamental role ascribed to such a move in recent theology is a significant development and prompts the question whether it constitutes a way particularly appropriate to the needs of our present situation. With that question in mind, I will look briefly at the way in which this approach has been worked out by three major theologians of recent years.

Karl Rahner's starting point is to ask, What is involved in our historical existence as human selves? Any answer we might give to that question must inevitably be based on the particular human experiences that have come our way. Rahner's goal, however, is to use those experiences to lay bare something that is to be distinguished from the particular, contingent experiences themselves – namely, the underlying realities or structures of existence that make any distinctively human experiences possible. How can this be done? Suppose we put to ourselves the question, What constitutes us the particular persons that we are? We can call on a variety of factors to provide information towards an answer: for example, knowledge of our genetic inheritance and of the environment in which we have been brought up and now live. Nevertheless, any answers of this kind only serve to pose more questions. The more we recognize the significance of our origins, genetic and environmental, the more puzzling become our apparent freedom and our sense of responsibility for what we make or fail to make of that inheritance. To deny that we have any such freedom or responsibility is not merely to go against a fundamental aspect of our experience; it is to deny what is most distinctively human about us. We cannot get away from the question of how we are able to contribute to shaping what is apparently given to us in our origins. How is it that we can 'make something of ourselves'? Reflection on these questions is likely to lead to the conclusion that, inescapable as they are, they are incapable of being answered, because any answer arising from within the system of acquiring knowledge with which we have to work is bound to generate yet further questions. Thus we are forced on into an awareness of the 'infinite question which encompasses us',[4] a question that can be described either as unanswerable or as its own answer.

This inescapable road of 'self-transcendence' shows us that human life has an ineluctable 'orientation towards mystery', and that God is the name for that 'absolute mystery' towards which this distinctively human style of reflection inevitably points. Rahner's appeal is not just to occasions of profound solitary introspection. It is to something that underlies the whole range of human and, therefore, social life: for example, to that which is implicit in such experiences as the unconditional character of love given or love received and the sense of responsibility for one's actions in what is apprehended as an absolute moral imperative. At the heart of all these distinctively human experiences are indications of an all-embracing and inconceivable mystery. I have described the process of reflection that can give rise to awareness of that mystery in highly intellectual terms (even if not in as sophisticated intellectual terms as Rahner employs), but Rahner insists that the experience itself is not dependent for its reality on such intellectual formulation. He argues that it should be recognized as present, as a form of 'unthematic awareness', even in the most rudimentary forms of genuinely human experience. Primitive burial customs, for example, are evidence of the presence of such awareness long before it was ever spelled out in any reasoned form.

The writings of Wolfhart Pannenberg reveal many emphases closely parallel to those we have outlined from Rahner's work. Pannenberg finds the distinctive difference between humans and the rest of the animal creation in the anthropological concept of 'openness to the world'. He sees it as 'the condition for man's experience of the world', and insists (in terms closely akin to Rahner's account of the never-ending quest of self-transcendence) that it is an openness 'beyond every experience and beyond every given situation . . . beyond a man's picture of the world at any given time . . . beyond every possible picture of the world and beyond the search for pictures of the world as such, as essential as this search may be'.[5] Again like Rahner, he lays great stress on the significance of freedom. Atheist critics of the notion of God have often argued that any concept of God the lawgiver is unacceptable precisely because of the implicit restriction of human freedom involved in it. For Pannenberg, however, that argument relies on a superficial understanding both of God and of human freedom. Moreover, he is not content simply to refute it; he stands it on its head. Only a transfinite reality, namely, God, makes real freedom possible.[6] Important as both these themes are in Pannenberg's thought, however, neither of them is its most characteristic feature. Pannenberg's particular emphasis falls on another aspect of what it is to be human, namely, hope. It seems, at first hearing, a most unlikely aspect of human living on which to focus attention in this context; particular hopes, as Pannenberg is well aware, may be mere delusions. Recalling once more the historical nature of our existence as human beings, however, he claims that hope as such is fundamental to human existence. It plays a decisive role in the distinctively human function of giving meaning to our lives.

Hope takes many forms. Hope for the future is an essential aspect of what gives purpose to our present work or to the upbringing of a family. Its range can extend much further in time and in scope, taking in both individual hopes for life after death and the Marxist hope for the social revolution that ushers in utopia. Our individual and social lives, however, are set in the context of a universal history. There are no cutoff points at which the search for meaning can rest content. A hope for universal fulfillment cannot, therefore, be dismissed as delusive in principle because it is postulated by the crucial role hope already plays in our lives now. Because that hope cannot be eliminated from life without destroying the distinctively human function of the search for meaning, we are motivated to postulate a goal for human history; in other words, we are motivated to postulate the reality of God and of the eschatological kingdom of God.

My third example is the work of Schubert Ogden. In his analysis of our existence as human selves, Ogden's emphasis is laid on the role of morality. Implicit in our behaviour as moral beings, he argues, is a basic confidence in the worthwhileness of existence. Ultimately, he claims, the only alternative to the assumption that existence is worthwhile is the 'Absurd Hero' of Albert Camus; and Camus' own insistent call for heroic resistance against the essential absurdity of human life is evidence of the self-contradictory character of the claim of life's meaninglessness. Ogden is well aware that there are happy and moral atheists, free of angst and keen to deny the conclusion he asserts. Nevertheless, that is not in itself argument against that conclusion; we often fail to recognize the implications of things that we take for granted and that are also fundamental to our lives. It is evidence, rather, of the need for careful philosophical reflection. Such reflection on our moral experience (as, indeed, on other aspects of human life) leads us to see, Ogden claims, that a sense of the worthwhileness of things and a confidence in life's ultimate meaning are necessary conditions for specifically human existence. It is, as he puts it, the one really essential 'proof of God's existence'.[7] The quotation marks around 'proof of God's existence' are, however, original and crucial. Ogden's conclusion is no return to the discredited understanding of theistic proofs. It is not a claim that there is, after all, a way of demonstrating the reality of God by some form of external or abstract reasoning. It is rather the claim that the reality of God is something that can, by a process of deep and careful reflection, come to be seen to be genuinely entailed in our practical existence as human selves.

I have taken these three as representative of many twentieth-century theologians who have followed a similar line of reasoning. Does that approach constitute that third way for which Kaufman asks? Before trying to answer that question, some preparatory comments are called for. The three theologians come from very different philosophical traditions. Behind Rahner stands a particular form of neo-Kantianism, specifically, that of Joseph Marechal. Pannenberg draws extensively on the complex patterns of Hegelian thought. Ogden works with a carefully articulated form of process metaphysics, deriving from the work of Charles Hartshorne. Is it possible to reflect in any useful way on all three together, without first examining each individually in the context of his own chosen metaphysic? Such analyses would certainly add to our illumination, and the thought of all three has indeed been subjected to such scrutiny. It would still be important, however, not to miss the forest for the trees. It is my contention that, for all their diversity, there is an agreement in fundamental strategy at the point on which I am concentrating attention. The measure of validity that can properly be allowed to that strategy is the issue at stake. It is true that the three emphasize different aspects of our humanity – Rahner knowledge, Pannenberg hope, Ogden morality. One might say that among them they develop the significances of the three theological virtues – faith, hope, and love. Those differences are, however, primarily a matter of emphasis. In each case, the overall appeal is to a broader range of human characteristics than the particular one on which I have concentrated attention. What all three have in common is that they find a grounding for their belief in God in what it is to be a human self.

In seeking to assess the validity of this general line of reasoning, we have first to ask what its role is. None of the theologians whose approach I have summarized attempts to re-establish the kind of argument for the existence of God that came under the hammer of David Hume's and Immanuel Kant's criticisms. And although each is a fully convinced Christian, none simply asserts the truth of Christian belief in God from within the sphere of his explicit Christian commitment. They do not fit within either the 'theoretical' or the 'fideistic' category, against both of which Kaufman warns us. The starting point from which they seek to develop their reflection is not what it is that makes possible specifically Christian experience but what it is that makes possible human experience as such. We have to ask if it is possible to speak of human existence in such universal terms, and, if it is, whether such universality points as firmly as they suggest in a theistic direction.

The emergence of historical consciousness has led us to emphasize the differences between ourselves and peoples of other cultures and of other ages. We are aware that there are many points at which there are deep differences in how we and they experience the world, because the world that we experience is a world of inherited meanings, which change over time in decisive ways. All this has made us highly suspicious of claims to speak in terms of a universal human nature, claims that were a common feature of much earlier philosophical and religious thought. This is something of which Rahner is acutely conscious. Our present forms of experience are not at the root of his argument, for these necessarily have a contingent and conditioned character about them, which makes it illegitimate to treat them as if of universal significance. His concern is with what he calls 'existentials', that which makes any form of human experience possible. That which is common to humankind is, for Rahner, precisely our historical existence as human selves. Nevertheless, although this may reassure us that he is unlikely to succumb to the danger of universalizing what is only a specific contemporary form of human experience, it is no guarantee that he will succeed in delineating what necessarily underlies human experience. The danger is not merely the risk of universalizing one's own form of experience; disputes between anthropologists suggest that it is also possible falsely to universalize what is apprehended of a culture very different from one's own. There is, indeed, no guarantee that we can rightly discern what is essential to human existence. It seems clear that we can, however, by a process of empathy, achieve some genuine understanding of cultures other than our own, and we cannot prescribe in advance any limit to how far that process may take us. It is not unreasonable, therefore, to attempt to clarify what is to be regarded as fundamental to human existence, provided we acknowledge the inevitably uncertain character of any particular account we may give.

If we accept the propriety of that first stage in the line of reasoning we are reviewing – namely, offering some delineation of what it is to be human – we have then to consider what kind of an argument can be built on it. It may help to begin with a nontheistic example. A traditional theme of philosophical discussion has been the grounds for the rejection of solipsism, traditionally spoken of as the problem concerning the existence of other minds. Belief in the existence of other minds is, indeed, a basic belief that we do not normally feel ourselves called upon to justify. If we do try to give reasons for that belief in the form of an inductive inference from the behaviour responses of others towards us, philosophers then delight in exposing the formal weaknesses in the argument propounded. It would be equally absurd, however, to suggest that our belief was some kind of arbitrary decision on our part. A more appropriate account would be to claim that the belief is already implicit in the formulation of the question, because the formulation of the question requires language and language is an essentially communal activity; it can only develop in a communal setting. The communal nature of language means that the existence of other persons is already demonstrated by our ability to raise the question of their existence at all. Indeed, the argument can be taken a stage further. Not only the existence of the other person but also the basic trustworthiness of the other are already given, because the possibility of communication presumes not only the existence of another but also that other's overall trustworthiness. Deceit and lying exist, but they are parasitic on trustworthiness. If they, not trustworthiness, were the norm, language would have been unable to develop as the form of communication that it is.

Ogden's formulation of the enterprise on which he sees himself engaged makes absolutely clear not only that it is not to be understood as basing itself on specific Christian insights but also that it is of the form that I have illustrated by the example of the argument against solipsism. In seeking to counter secularist negations, his appeal is not to any kind of supernaturalism but to 'a secularity which has become fully self-conscious and which therefore makes explicit the faith in God already implied in what it affirms'.[8] If the fact of language implies the general trustworthiness of humankind, because it could not have emerged or continue to function on any other basis, then the fact of morality, it is claimed, could not have arisen or continued to be practised without a confidence in the ultimate worth of life. God is a name for that which calls forth this all-embracing confidence.

Two questions need to be asked of this argument and of the parallel affirmations of God as the answer to the infinite question that encompasses us or as the ground of a universal goal to human history. The first question is whether that is the only way of reading our human experience. Granted that the experience to which the argument appeals is human experience as such, not special Christian experience, may not the way of reading the experience nonetheless have been decisively, if unconsciously, influenced by a person's specifically Christian experience? There is no conclusive way of answering that question. Undoubtedly, for those who argue in these terms, their particular understanding of what is involved in being human is an integral element in their Christian faith. In so far as it is appropriate to speak of a causal connection between the two at all, however, it seems just as reasonable to claim that it is the sense of such an underlying confidence (not necessarily clearly articulated at first) that has led to their adoption of Christian beliefs as to see the connection the other way round. There is certainly no more circularity in this argument than is inescapably present in all reflections of so foundational a character.

The second question is whether the line of reflection we have been following requires us to assert that the infinite question is also an answer or to speak of that which calls forth an all-embracing confidence. Might it not instead be that, in the course of evolution, we have simply devised such conceptions for practical purposes? Kaufman has emphasized very strongly how it is our practical needs as 'active-choosing-creative beings', who 'must judge what confronts them and attempt to transform it in accordance with visions of what now is not', that have called forth our varied human conceptions of God.[9] The crucial role of human construction in Christian belief in God (as in the beliefs of other religions), on which Kaufman lays such stress, seems to me inescapable. Nevertheless, that by itself is, as he insists, neutral in relation to the question of the reality of the 'real' God, as contrasted with the 'available' God or gods of the particular religions.[10]

Does the issue, then, have to be left in that entirely undecided and undecidable state? It is worth considering the parallel debate between instrumentalists and critical realists in science. The naive realist's claim that the physical scientist can describe for us just what the external world is like is as untenable as the claim that our theological accounts are direct descriptions of the nature of God. The growing realization of the impossibility of a naive realist view of science prompted a swing by reaction towards an instrumentalist view. Could any objective reality be allowed to the concepts with which the scientist works? Was not their 'truth' simply a matter of their practical usefulness in helping us achieve our experimental and technical goals? There can be no question of any formal disproof of such a claim. Nevertheless, it would, indeed, be an odd and surely implausible position to maintain that our theoretical understanding of the world could then be so reliable in practical terms, if it bears no relation to how the world actually is. It is an argument that has found a good deal of support among philosophers of science in recent years. The fact that it has been dubbed the 'no miracles' argument should not discourage the theologian from adapting it to his or her purpose.[11] The same line of reasoning can be used to suggest that, if the concept of God is of such crucial practical significance as Kaufman claims, then it would be strange if it were nothing more than a useful instrument towards human living and corresponded in no way to the ultimate reality of how our world is.

Not all conceptions of God have had the positive pragmatic value that Kaufman ascribes to the underlying conception of a transcendent divine reality. If an argument of the kind that I have been pursuing lends any support to the validity of belief in God as such, then by the same token it calls for continuing and thoroughgoing criticism of the particular constructions through which that basic belief in God finds its expression. There can be little doubt that such criticisms will be intensified by those trends of thought that are said to be taking us out of the 'modern' into an uncharted 'postmodern' age. Theology will need to be attentive and responsive to those trends. Nevertheless, it should not be afraid that all the old landmarks are about to be swept away. What I have been trying to suggest is that, whatever form the discussion of such problems may take, as long as it remains a structured human discussion it will not fail to carry within itself (whatever the substance of the discussion) a seed with the potential of coming to flower as a well-rooted belief in God.

11

In What Contexts Does it Make Sense to Say, 'God Acts in History'?

I first met Schubert Ogden in 1977. It was my first visit to the United States and he had invited me to come to Dallas. I arrived in his office at 9.30 in the morning to find an array of my writings, heavily underscored, open on his desk. After three hours of vigorous theological exchange, I extricated myself to keep a luncheon engagement. His concluding remark was 'When are you coming back for some more?' So began a personal friendship and theological interchange from which I have gained much – and would have gained much more, had the geographical distance between us allowed for more frequent meetings.

In my writings I have not often found myself wanting to make any direct retraction of things that I have written earlier. The nearest I have come to it was in an article on 'Farrer's Concept of Double Agency' where I wrote:

> It is precisely the notion of God's particular action that I find particularly difficult. I now think that in the past I have overreacted to those difficulties and written too exclusively of a divine purpose for the world and for mankind in general terms. I think that what I have said before can and should be extended to speak of particular divine purposes for individuals in their specific situations. But even to say that is still (ostensibly at least) to say a good deal less than is being said by talk of God's particular actions.[1]

The source of that change of heart was a conversation with Schubert Ogden in which he had vigorously challenged me with the need and possibility for the theologian to speak in such individual terms.

When the invitation to share in this well-deserved tribute arrived, I was just embarking on the preparation of a special course of lectures, later published as *God's Action in the World*.[2] That book owes a great deal to Schubert Ogden, for he is one of those who have most helped me through writing and through conversation in my struggles with this central but difficult topic. In the preparation of those lectures, I had to wrestle again with the issue of God's particular action, which had been the subject of that earlier conversation between us and about which he has written in so thought-provoking a manner in his essay 'What Sense Does it Make to Say "God Acts in History"?'[3]

Ogden begins that essay by justifying his choice of title in preference to an alternative form of the question, namely: 'Can one make sense of the statement "God acts in history"?' We ought not, he argues, to expect to be able to pronounce, as that way of posing the question suggests we can, between the possibility and impossibility of making sense of the statement – except by actually making some particular sense of it.[4] But his own formulation of the question could also suggest a sharper dichotomy than is appropriate – either succeeding or failing to make sense of the statement.

For we sometimes use the language of 'making sense' in a graded way. We speak of 'making good sense' or 'making some sort of sense'. So there are perhaps mediating forms in which the question might usefully be posed, such as: 'Is the sense it makes to say "God acts in history" such that we might reasonably prefer to express it in some other way?' That is a formulation with which Ogden himself might have some sympathy. For in speaking of Bultmann's doubt 'whether mythological statements make *theological* sense', he appends his own comment 'or, better said, whether they are an appropriate way of expressing the sense or meaning that theological statements are supposed to express'.[5] Moreover, his own affirmation that 'God's action, in its fundamental sense, is not an action in history at all'[6] suggests that there could be grounds for saying something similar about the inappropriateness, though not the vacuity, of speaking of God's action in history – despite his own unequivocal conclusion that the historical event of Jesus' life and ministry 'stands before us as itself God's act in a sense that we both can and *must* affirm'.[7]

We also speak of things making sense in one context but not in another. To say that 'stars in their courses fought against Sisera' (Judg. 5.20) makes good sense in a song of victory, but it would make no sense in a treatise on astronomy, even though there is no equivocation in the use of the word 'stars'. So there is another formulation of the question, which again encourages the expectation of a more qualified, but still positive, answer to the underlying question, namely: 'In what contexts does it make sense to say "God acts in history"?' And it is this formulation that I have chosen for the title of this essay.

The most obvious contrast of contexts within which we might want to speak of God acting in history is that between religious and theological utterance. The difference between the two is not absolute. Most religious utterances embody, albeit often uncon- sciously, the fruit of some prior theological reflection, and theological reflection can be carried out in a variety of ways, some more and some less distanced from the forms of direct religious utterance. Nonetheless there is an important difference between the two, not altogether unlike the difference between the two contexts in the case of the stars. Religious utterance uses the vigorous and concrete imagery characteristic of the song-writer or the poet. The theologian seeks to clarify, coordinate, and work out the implications of this basic religious awareness, as the astronomer seeks to clarify, coordinate, and work out the implications of the varied human observations of the stars. The idiom appropriate to the more reflective task is very different from that appropriate to the more immediate and primary activity.

The work in which both Ogden and I have been engaged has been firmly at the theological end of the spectrum. And the theological answers that we have given to the question of how to understand the language of God's action are very similar in structure, even though we operate with significantly different analyses of action. Ogden allows three senses in which one may speak of God acting. First, as we have already seen, there is the fundamental sense which transcends history, 'whereby he [God] ever and again actualizes his own divine essence by responding in love to all the creatures in his world'.[8] Second, 'every creature is to some extent God's act – just as, by analogy, all our bodily actions are to some extent our actions as selves'.[9] And third, 'there are certain distinctively human words and deeds in which his [God's] characteristic action as Creator and Redeemer is appropriately re-presented or revealed'; these are in a special sense 'acts of God analogously to the way in which our outer acts *are* our acts insofar as they re-present our own characteristic decisions as selves or persons'.[10] I have not found it so congenial to distinguish those inner decisions whereby we constitute our own selves and regard them as the primary form of human action. Working rather with an understanding of action as 'a piece of intentional behaviour initiated by an agent', I have nonetheless proposed a similar threefold structure for the understanding of divine action: first, a fundamental sense in which there is only one act of God, namely the continuing creation of the universe; second, the regular patterns according to which the physical world operates, which by their very constitution are elements within the divine activity but not, in my judgment, to be spoken of as distinguishable acts of God in themselves; and, third, actions by human agents, who freely intend to further the purposes of God, seek God's grace to enable them to do so, and do in fact achieve their intended goal, which may in a secondary and highly qualified sense be allowed the designation 'acts of God'.[11] I do not intend to argue here the relative merits of these two ways of conceiving action in attempting an interpretation of God's acts. That has been interestingly done in comparisons of Ogden and Kaufman, to whom on this issue I stand much closer.[12] I want rather to stress the measure of substantive agreement between us, and go on to consider the implications of such a theological understanding for the actual use of the language of God's action in its original, that is to say, its religious, context.

The primary task of theological reflection is to understand and clarify existing religious usage. Often it will have achieved its goal if it leads to modifications in the way in which the traditional religious language is understood. But its outcome need not always be to leave things where they were linguistically. Its reflections may point to particular religious contexts within which certain widely accepted forms of religious language are inappropriate, misleading, or straightforwardly false. Is that the case in this instance? Does the theological analysis give the language of God's action in history a clean bill of health and underwrite its use in all circumstances? Or does it suggest the desirability of some modification in the way it is used or some restriction on the contexts in which it is employed?

The first issue that I want to consider is the fact that there is one class of special divine action clearly affirmed in scripture for which our theological analyses allow no place. The Assyrian is the rod of God's anger; it is God who sends him and bids him spoil and plunder the land of Israel (Isa. 10.5–6). Similarly, it is God who gives Cyrus the victories that lead to the restoration of Israel and the rebuilding of Jerusalem (Isa. 44.28–45.3). These are as clear and as significant examples of God being said to act in history as any to be found in scripture. Yet the action of the Assyrian warlord can hardly be said to re-present the characteristic action of God as Creator and Redeemer whereby he continually responds in love to all the creatures in the world. The Assyrians' intention is explicitly described as an evil intention for mass-destruction (Isa. 10.7–8). Nor can Cyrus be said to be aiming to further God's purpose or to be seeking his grace to do so. He is explicitly stated to have no knowledge of God (Isa. 45.4). If the imperialistic adventures of the Assyrians and the Babylonians were done in response to the lure of the divine love, then God employs the principle that the end justifies the means in a way more cynical than that of the most cynical of politicians.

Does our inability to make theological sense of the scriptural accounts of God's action in relation to the Assyrians or to Cyrus mean that we should abandon all talk of God acting in history in such cases? If we can make no sense of the statements theologically, then it does surely follow that they should have no place in our theological speech. But that does not necessarily mean that the language was being improperly used in the first instance. It is no coincidence that so much of Hebrew prophecy (including both the passages that we have been discussing) is in the form of poetic diction. Nor does it necessarily mean that such language should have no place in any contemporary equivalent of the prophetic context. The aim of such prophetic language is to bring home to its hearers the seriousness of the situation that they are in and its potentiality for a response that will significantly re-present God's action or forward God's purposes. There is no lack of contemporary examples (the inner-city riots in Britain at the time at which this is being written is an obvious one) which call for that kind of prophetic interpretation. To speak of them in terms of what God is doing and saying to us in history is a legitimate form of such speech.

But what is the reflective theologian to make of it? Austin Farrer uses the description of the Assyrian as the rod of God's anger as an example of his concept of 'double agency'. He reflects on how the ancient prophet may have conceived 'the mechanism of the divine control' as lying 'in the openness of men's thoughts to pressures of which they are unaware'. But in the end he concludes that the Hebrew prophet and the modern Christian stand together. They can be sure the Assyrian action is a 'divine effect'. But they neither can, nor need, know anything about 'the causal joint (so to speak) between infinite and finite action' because such knowledge 'can play no part in our concern with God and his will'.[13] There may be contexts in which this combination of strong affirmation of the fact and reverent, but total, agnosticism of the mechanism or manner of its operation is appropriate. But this is not one of them. If a theological analysis of the kind that both Ogden and I have put forward is on the right lines, we ought to be prepared to say that the language of divine action in a case like that of the Assyrians is not to be taken to imply that the Assyrian action is a 'divine effect' in anything more than that limited sense in which everything that happens is a divine effect. There is no hidden causal joint, not even a 'causal joint (so to speak)'. If religious devotion can flourish without knowing the manner by which the divine effect is supposed to be achieved, it can get on fine without affirming that it is a specific divine effect at all. The prophetic language has an altogether different rationale.

This distinction between prophecy and theology is not without its own difficulties. As was recognized at the outset, the frontier between religious and theological speech cannot be drawn in an absolute or clear-cut way. Theologies of liberation provide an example of just such a difficult, borderline case. As Ogden himself has expressed it, such 'theologies typically are not so much theology as witness'.[14] Such a remark is descriptive rather than evaluative. Theology is not superior to witness; the difference is one of function. The claim, made to me in conversation by one American theologian, that 'all theology should be prophetic theology' only holds true in so far as we also allow that 'all prophecy should be theological prophecy'. To demand such a union of the two in practice is a false, utopian demand. What we should be striving for is not their conflation or their identity, but a recognition of their mutual interdependence and therefore of the importance of their listening to each other. For the present we are better served by acknowledging the need for both direct prophetic proclamation and sustained critical reflection. Despite the existence of borderline cases, we need the variety of their different vocations with their different vocabularies.

The concept of 'vocation' suggests another, smaller-scale aspect of our central problem. History is not a matter only of battles and royal decrees, of the decisions of warlords and emperors. It is a matter also, as a good deal of modern historical writing emphasizes, of the more ordinary lives of individual men and women. So any sense that we are to make of God acting in history must relate not only to the broader sweep of historical development but also to the lives of individuals.

In secular usage 'vocation' is a dead metaphor. How its significance is understood in religious usage is more uncertain. It is not always clear whether someone using the term in that context understands it in some quite literal sense or at least intends the metaphor to be taken as a living one, implying something more than would be intended in secular usage. There are two components which might go to make up that something more. First there is the conviction that there is a particular role or purpose which God has for me to fulfil. Secondly there is the further point of there being some specific call whereby God has

made or is making known to me what his will for me is. In other
words, in addition to God's particular will for me, there may also
be some particular action of God whereby he communicates that
will to me, though not in a way that removes my freedom to
refuse. Many biblical stories speak of such a particular will, and
indeed the communication of it, as preceding even the birth of the
person concerned. Such accounts cannot be taken at their face
value. To do so would involve far too predetermined a conception both of the way we grow as human persons and of the
circumstances within which any lifework will have to be played
out in the future. Such language can only coherently be understood as a vivid way of expressing retrospectively the significance
of a person's life in relation to God's purpose in the world.[15] But
those objections do not apply in the same way to the concept of
God having a particular purpose for me now. That is a concept, as
I acknowledged earlier, which Ogden has helped persuade me
must not be eliminated from the theologian's purview. But I still
have difficulty in determining just what the theologian ought to
make of it. How, then, is it to be understood in relation to
vocation?

To speak of God's particular purpose for me now may suggest
that there is one, and only one, specific way in which my life can
be lived in line with the will of God. The use of language about
testing whether a person 'really has a vocation or not' (regularly
used in relation to the ordained ministry or the religious life)
easily lends itself to that sort of interpretation. It can sound as if
we are trying to decide between two possibilities: either the
person has been called, in which case he or she must be ordained,
or the person has not been called, in which case he or she must not
be ordained. But it does not need to be and should not be
understood in that way. It smacks too much of a divinely
preprogrammed destiny. There are normally a variety of ways in
which our lives could be lived in line with the will of God. Testing
a vocation is the process of trying to determine whether the
proposed course of action is or is not one such way. Similarly the
idea of a particular divine 'call' may suggest that we ought to give
extra weight to any unusual inner experiential evidence, over and
above the criteria that might usually be employed for determining

appropriateness for the proposed work. An inner conviction about what decision to make may arise intuitively and unexpectedly in any walk of life, without involving any particular religious understanding or implications. The concept of a particular divine call ought not to be allowed to give any additional significance to that sort of experience. Many great wrongs, as a book like William James' *Varities of Religious Experience* vividly illustrates, have been done through failure to heed that danger.

If the language of vocation, when treated as something more than a dead metaphor, has such inherent dangers, what is its value? The question needs to be answered on the basis of our theological analysis of the concept of God's action. Seen in that light it serves primarily as a forceful reminder of the setting within which our lives are lived. We live in a world in which God is continually active as creator and redeemer, a world of whose existence he is the purposive initiator and continuator. And it is in relation to this continually God-given reality, with its rich range of future possibilities, that any determination of our own actions needs to be seen. Moreover, it is what we understand to be the character and goal of that divine action, as we see them represented in Christ, that should provide the criteria of our choosing. To allow the language of vocation to become an utterly dead metaphor would be to weaken that all-important religious context within which our lives are to be lived and our choices to be made.

The language of vocation, therefore, remains important, but it is equally important that its continuation goes hand in hand with critical reflection about its proper understanding. And such reflection may lead us to suggest that within religious usage there are different contexts within some of which it is appropriate to talk of 'what God is calling us to do' or of 'what the Holy Spirit is showing us to be the will of God,' and other contexts in which such language cannot properly be used. I can best indicate the kind of distinction I have in mind by reference to an aspect of moral discourse discussed by Stephen Toulmin in his book *The Place of Reason in Ethics*. Toulmin distinguishes between the appropriate contexts for the deontologist's appeal to moral principles and the utilitarian's consideration of consequences. In reasoning about the rightness of particular actions in normal circumstances, the former reasoning is appropriate. In that context, 'because it was a promise' is a sufficient answer; to offer any further, more general reason would be out of place. Consideration of consequences is appropriate in contexts where there is a conflict between accepted principles or where a generally agreed social practice is called into question. The two different kinds of reasoning are seen not as conflicting rival explanations for the same situation but as appropriate in different contexts.[16] May not something similar be true also in the case that we are considering?

I have argued that the significance of the language of divine vocation lies in its reminder of the wider setting in relation to which our decisions are to be made and of the criterion for making such decisions provided by the Christian understanding of God's continuing action as creator and redeemer. To ask 'What is the will of God for me?' or 'What is the Holy Spirit saying to me?' is a way of ensuring that our deliberations are pursued in that full context. Such phrases cannot properly be used to justify the particular decision reached. They make no sense as justifying reasons for particular decisions – even about our choice of vocation. That has to be done in terms of the particular criteria for decision which our reflection on the nature of God's action has led us to adopt in the particular case. The Council of Jerusalem (or the author of the Book of Acts, if he is the real originator of the phrase) has a lot to answer for when it employed the words 'It is the decision of the Holy Spirit, and our decision . . .' (Acts 15.29). For if that is intended as a reason why the Gentile churches should accept the decisions of the council, it smacks more of authoritarian manipulation than of acceptable religious reasoning. It is even more dangerous as paving the way for claims about the inerrancy of councils, so rightly contradicted by the Articles of the Church of England.[17] The action of the Holy Spirit makes sense as a reminder of the full context of Christian decision-making or as a justification of the general style of such decision-making. It does not make sense as a reason for particular decisions.

The kind of reflection that I have been pursuing here in relation to prophetic affirmation of God's hand in an Assyrian invasion or an inner-city riot and in relation to the understanding of 'vocation' could be widely extended. There are hardly any aspects of Christian religious practice itself, or of Christian understanding of the world, in which the language of God's action is not both central and problematic. An obvious further example that I have discussed elsewhere is the practice of prayer.[18]

But the purpose of this essay is not so much to solve such problems as to make a plea for serious engagement with them. The most sophisticated theological reflection and the most ordinary forms of religious practice need to be carried on in conscious relationship to one another. For me one of the most significant features of Schubert Ogden's work has been his determination to combine the two. Few theologians have attacked the problems facing them with the same measure of unrelenting rational inquiry, and few theologians have been more concerned about the implications of that inquiry for ordinary religious practice. Without that dual commitment our theology runs the risk of sterility and our religious practice that of the corrupting suspicion of bad faith. What our theological analysis of how and where it makes sense to say 'God acts in history' implies for religious practice needs more careful and thorough exploration than it commonly receives.

12

Can We Still Do Christology?

On 1 May 1990, Lee Keck read a paper to a seminar in Oxford on the christology of Matthew. I came away from it with an epigrammatic phrase from his paper firmly lodged in my mind. Four days later I had to read a paper to a seminar on how a contemporary theologian can best approach the topic of christology. Lee Keck's epigram helped to focus my thoughts. Another four days later came a totally unexpected but very welcome invitation to contribute to a Festschrift for him. My task seemed clearly laid out for me. What else could I do but try to develop that which his stimulus had so recently helped to bring to birth, even though my reflections on his words, pursued in relation to a very different set of problems, might have led me in ways along which he had not himself wished to direct me.

In a very general introduction to his paper, Lee Keck had begun by defining christology as the attempt to give expression to the relation of Jesus to God, and he had gone on to draw the traditional distinction between the person and the work of Christ: 'The former makes the latter a possibility; the latter makes the former a necessity.' At first hearing, it sounds rather grander to be a necessity than merely a possibility. And at one level that is clearly an intended implication of the epigram. In the order of being, a priority is ascribed to the person over what that person does. It is his relation to God, the unique status of who he is, that makes Christ's work possible – that is, that enables it to exist. But that reflection only serves to remind us that there is another level where to be a necessity confers no such automatic priority. In the order of knowing, it is the fruit of Christ's work which is the more accessible to us and from which we have to begin. Christ's personal status, his unique relation to God, may be that without which his work would not be possible. But that fact carries with it no guarantee that we will have access to knowledge of that relation; it does not ensure our ability to speak of it in a way that would constitute a doctrine of the person of Christ. His relation to God may be necessary to his work in the order of being; it does not follow that giving an account of it will necessarily prove a possibility for us. On the face of it that is an alarming suggestion, for christology has normally been seen – in line with the structure of the principal Christian creeds – as the central doctrine of Christian faith. But once raised, the difficulty needs to be faced. It cannot be dealt with by a refusal to admit that it exists.

There is nothing peculiar to theology about this link between work and person. Any action statement necessarily implies an agent; a 'person' statement is therefore implicit in every 'action' statement. A statement about the writing of a book, for example, logically implies that there are statements that can be made about an author, even if we may not always be in a position to make them. If we know who the author is, the 'person' statement we choose to make will depend on the context within which and the purpose for which we are making it. We are not normally likely to feel it appropriate to retail the author's biography in every detail. To a typist trying to decipher a difficult manuscript, it might be significant to be told that the author was left-handed; to a reviewer trying to understand the book's approach to its subject, it might help to be told that the author was a Yale professor. Similar 'person' statements may also be made, sometimes indeed with great confidence, on the basis of inference, even where the personal identity of the author is not known. Statements of that kind, though drawn entirely from the evidence of the work itself, may still be of use in elucidating aspects of the work other than those that were the basis of the inference. Absolute certainty, however, as contrasted with practical certitude, can only arise where the work is one that cannot logically be performed by anybody other than the agent or kind of agent inferred. I can assert, for example, with total and unqualified certainty that the person who appointed me Regius Professor of Divinity was the reigning British monarch, because only the monarch has the necessary authority to appoint a Regius Professor. Or, again, when people receive sacramental absolution in a Catholic church, the one giving it (even though he may remain entirely hidden) can be known necessarily to be a priest. Our absolute confidence arises from the fact that in the case of those particular works, only one person, or one kind of person, is entitled to fulfil the role of agent. Even if someone else were to do the same things and say the same words, they would not be performing the same 'action', because what they did would not constitute an 'appointment' or an act of 'sacramental absolution'.

Other examples could be added extending the range of different possible relationships between what we affirm about particular works or actions and what can appropriately be said about the person doing that work or performing that action. But these will be sufficient to suggest how varied are the kinds of interrelation that it may be useful to bear in mind when considering the connection between the work and the person of Christ. But before we seek to apply what has been said so far to the substantive issue of christology, there is one other preliminary line of reflection I want to pursue.

On the analogy of the traditional division of christological ideas into person and work, I have been talking about person statements as contrasted with statements about work or actions. And my concern so far has been with the relationships between those two kinds of statements. But one might also draw distinctions between the kinds of person statements that we make. As the examples given show, some might deal with particular physical characteristics (e.g., being left-handed), others with an office held (e.g., Yale professor or Catholic priest). Such statements are either trivial or relatively external. Being a Yale professor implies that someone has been granted tenure by the appropriate committee on the basis of books written and other duties performed; being a Catholic priest implies that some-one has been ordained by a bishop, after going through a required process of training. Those offices may, of course, imply a good deal more than that. The holding of such an office may be part of that person's self-conception, an essential element in any answer he or she would give to the question, Who am I? The kind of answer that might be given to that more existential question is perhaps the most obvious type of statement suggested by the concept of a person statement. In most cases it will not be very different from a selective account of that person's work or actions. Our own understanding of our significance as persons is normally linked very closely with the nature of our relationship with those close to us and the role that we play in society more widely. When a person's self-understanding is less closely related to his or her public role, it may be difficult to infer it from that person's actions. It may take the form of a more private, autobiographical statement needing rather different kinds of evidence. Indeed, even written autobiographical evidence would need to be treated with care, since a written autobiography is normally designed (consciously or unconsciously) to project a particular understanding of a person, which he or she wants to convey to the reader, but which may not correspond entirely with that person's own most profound self-understanding.

None of the examples I have given so far incorporates the distinctive character of traditional statements about the person of Christ, which Lee Keck spoke of as the relation of Jesus to God. That dimension is one that is likely to figure quite often in the context of an autobiographical statement, in relation to the question, Who am I? But it could also figure in a more third-person account arising out of a person's work. Someone might well be described as the gift of God to his or her generation, or as the divinely-inspired prophet raised up by God to meet the needs of the moment. The fact that we have no autobiographical evidence to start from may make statements about the relation of Jesus to God difficult to establish, but it does not make them impossible.

The theologian who wishes to make christological statements of this kind in a responsible way must begin by reflecting on the purpose for which they are being made and the evidence on which it is possible to base them. To say that the person of Christ is the necessary foundation for his work suggests that we are in search of affirmations of an objective and ontological kind that will serve as a foundation stone for all subsequent affirmations about the work of Christ. Traditional statements about the eternal consubstantial relation of the Son to the Father and the co-existence of full divine and human natures in the one person of Christ sound like statements of that kind and reinforce our aspiration to make appropriate affirmations of the same sort for our own time. But are we in a position where such aspirations are open to fulfilment?

If what we are aspiring to give is an account of Jesus' relation to God, any such account is bound to be influenced by (as well as to influence) our prior understanding of God. What seems to me clear both from the history of theology and from philosophical reflection (though it is not in fact an uncontroversial claim) is that there is an anthropological component in every doctrine of God. That is not to say that all doctrines of God are arbitrary expressions of human subjectivity. It is to assert that the particular forms of their expression are inevitably and quite properly coloured by the concerns that impinge on us as particularly significant or problematic. Traditionally minded Western theologians (whether liberal or conservative) are usually aware enough that this is the case with respect to political, liberation, feminist, or African theologians. They may welcome such theologies and the distinctive christologies that are a part of them, but they will almost certainly go on to point out at the same time that the very specific direction of their dominant concern is a source not only of strength, but also of limitation and one-sidedness. But they are having to learn that they themselves are no exception to this general rule. Statements about the person of Christ are bound to be affected in this way. But to say that is only to recall and to emphasize the partial and existential character of all theological statements. In relation to our immediate discussion, it implies that statements about the person of Christ will not only be, in part at least, derived from the work of Christ, but that the form they take will be influenced by whatever aspect of human life in relation to God is of dominant concern to us.

As we go on to consider the evidence on which affirmations about the person of Christ have to be based, the difficulty of separating out statements about his person and his work becomes more acute. In its broadest terms that evidence is the whole complex of the Christian tradition. For the purpose of evaluating the evidence, that complex can be broken down into separable factors in a number of different ways. But however that separation is done, those factors remain part of a whole, always operative in combination with one another and not in isolation. Anglicans have traditionally spoken of the threefold cord of scripture, tradition, and reason. Its operations, like those of the Trinity itself, are undivided. We cannot come to scripture unaffected by the subsequent tradition that has helped to form us, nor can we draw anything from it without the help of reasoned reflection; tradition is itself a form of reasoned reflection on scripture; and reason cannot directly tell us about Christian faith without making use of the content of both scripture and tradition. More recent developments in theology suggest that that particular analysis is not perhaps the most useful framework to follow. I propose to assess the evidence under a fourfold scheme: 1. historical evidence about Jesus for which scripture is, of course, the primary but not the sole source; 2. the direct witness of scripture as the canonical document of the church; 3. tradition, in the form of authoritative church teaching; and 4. tradition as a still continuing stream of transformative religious experience.

1. *History*

Critical study has made clear what the church has almost always known, but not so often explicitly acknowledged, namely, that the scriptural accounts of Jesus are not straightforwardly historical in character. Whether that is a matter of serious concern for faith as a whole may be open to dispute. What ought not to be open to dispute is that it has serious consequences for a doctrine of the person of Christ, understood as one that seeks to give expression to the relation of Jesus to God. I stated earlier that at the human level one of the most significant forms of evidence for such an enterprise would be autobiographical statements of an existential character. In the past, Christians have often believed themselves to have access to just such statements in the 'I am' sayings of the Fourth Gospel. They are, for example, the linchpin of Liddon's very precisely articulated doctrine of the person of

Christ in his famous Bampton lectures.[1] Today, scholarly consensus would deny that the words can properly be taken to have that historical autobiographical character. That is not to deny them all christological significance whatever, but it is to alter the nature of that significance.

And the implications of historical-critical study are, of course, much more far-reaching than just a relocation of the Johannine 'I am' sayings. The strongly interpretive character of all the gospel writings makes it notoriously difficult to discriminate between those things that are straightforwardly true of Jesus of Nazareth and those things ascribed to him as a result of the imaginative creativity of the evangelist or the corporate experience of his community. Once again that does not eliminate their significance, but it does alter the character of it. What might have been expected to provide the most direct evidence for speaking about the relation of *Jesus* to God turns out to be a source which cannot be used for that purpose with much confidence. One example of the difficulty of such an enterprise is the tour de force (in my judgment, the ultimately unsuccessful tour de force) of Wolfhart Pannenberg to develop a strong christology on the basis of the resurrection understood as an event whose truth can be affirmed in accordance with the canons of critical history.

2. *Scripture*

What has been said so far is not intended to deny that there is an underlying historical reality to the figure of Jesus that the Gospel records present to us. It is simply to emphasize the extreme difficulty of access to that reality, particularly in respect to his own understanding of his relation to God. The evidence of scripture, on the other hand, is directly accessible; it is there for us to read. Its interpretation is, of course, still open to dispute, but it is a less inherently speculative exercise than the attempt to get at some underlying historical basis. It is not surprising, therefore, that this approach should have proved very attractive to those who combine an acute critical sensitivity with a broadly conservative religious feeling. But the difficulty in using this evidence for our present enterprise is twofold. In the first place, the Jesus whose relation to God we would be describing would be the Jesus of the Christian scriptures, whose relation to Jesus of Nazareth is real but uncertain and problematic, particularly on the question of how his relation to God is to be understood. If the former, that is the Jesus of the Christian scriptures, whom we acknowledge to be in part the product of an imaginative literary creativity, is the real subject of christology, that would make a difference to the significance of our statements about him, particularly in respect to God's relation to the actualities of historical existence. It is not the same thing to ascribe incarnate status to a narrative, history-like Jesus and to ascribe it to Jesus of Nazareth.

But the second problematic aspect in using scriptural evidence holds us back even from this revised form of ascription. There is no single history-like Jesus to be found in the Gospel narratives. Mark and John may both speak of him as Son of God. But there is a world of difference between the enigmatic Son of God of Mark's Gospel, who struggles in Gethsemane to align his will with that of his heavenly Father, and the pre-existent Son of God who comes from above, from the bosom of the Father, to reveal the one whose glory he has shared since before the foundation of the world. The evidence of the Gospels as it bears on the relation of Jesus to God seems incurably diverse.

3. *The teaching of the tradition*

The general problem of the diversity of the scriptural evidence about Jesus is not new, though the particular way it impinges on us is. The emergence of an orthodox christology, finding particular expression at Nicaea and Chalcedon, was the outcome of wrestling with that diversity in the light of the church's experience of the life of faith. Some people have looked to the formal utterances of those councils as the proper starting point, the authoritative basis for our affirmations about the person of Christ. But it would be an odd procedure to adopt. They were dependent on the same sources of scripture and the subsequent experience of the church that are open to us. And they too were historically contingent in terms of both conceptual categories and political pressures. They are primary evidence for what the church has believed and taught. But for the relation of Jesus to God, their evidence is much more indirect. And the results of treating them as primary evidence for that latter question are even odder than the procedure of adopting them as such. Modern writers pursuing this approach are liable to recreate the kind of discussion that characterized the debates between monotheletes and dyotheletes in the seventh century. The logic of arguing from that approach leads Thomas Morris to describe Christ's relation to God in terms of his having two minds, one earthly and the other distinctively divine, with an asymmetric accessing relation between them.[2]

4. *The experience of the tradition*

I have already claimed that our experience of God is always, and rightly, a factor in determining the form of our theology. It is reasonable to see it as a more significant factor than is normally acknowledged in the theologies of those who place great emphasis on the objectivity of their method. But some theologians have been quite explicit about the prime role played by Christian experience in the determination of theology and, not least, of christology. In Paul Tillich's words, 'Christology is a function of soteriology.' It is the experience of the overcoming of the divide between essence and existence that assures us that that overcoming must have been decisively enacted somewhere at the origins of that stream of experience from which our own experience of overcoming derives. It is this experience that enables us to make certain affirmations about the Christ, even (as Tillich puts it) if we cannot be sure that his name was Jesus.[3] There is nothing logically incoherent in that. We have already aknowledged the existence of cases where quite firm affirmations can be made about the person lying behind a particular work, even though his identity remains unknown. But Tillich's remark is nonetheless a sharp reminder of how little such an approach will be able to provide if the affirmations we seek to make are really to be about the relation of Jesus to God.

Each of these sources of evidence for any christology could be – and, of course, has been – developed at far greater length and their significance weighed in more careful and detailed ways. My intention in this more impressionistic survey has been to reflect in very general terms on their strengths and weaknesses as grounds for the work of christology. But it would be wrong to pursue a policy of 'divide and conquer'; we would not be justified in pointing to the inherent difficulties in each considered in isolation and, on that basis alone, ruling out the possibility of any christology of a traditional kind. Indeed the criticisms briefly outlined in the preceding discussion are essentially criticisms of attempts to establish a christology too exclusively on the basis of one type of evidence. The various types of evidence, as I have emphasized already, do not come to us in isolation but in tight-knit combination. And taken conjointly, they constitute a powerful case for strong and positive affirmations about the figure of Christ. But the cumulative case that they constitute is one that enables us to say things about the impact of the coming of Christ rather than about the individual figure of Jesus. If that is the true nature of the evidence on which any christology is appropriately to be based, its natural form would seem to be an understanding of the Christ-event in the context of an overall theology, rather than an understanding of the person of Jesus in his relation to God.

Is there then no way in which we can work back, behind those affirmations about the Christ-event to which the converging strands of evidence direct us, and say something more specifically about the relation of Jesus to God as the underlying reality that made that event and its consequences possible? In our preliminary survey of everyday links between works and persons, we noted some cases where the character of the work in question provided incontrovertible evidence about the nature of the agent. An argument of that kind has commonly been used in the past (and remains influential still) to enable a move behind statements about Christ's work to statements about his person. It is a line of reasoning applied both to particular stories in the Gospels and, more broadly, to the later experience of the church. Only God, it may be said, can give the forgiveness which Jesus pronounces so directly over the paralytic; only a fully divine saviour can effect the salvation that the church experiences in Christ. But God's forgiveness is not formalized or institutionalized in the way that the church's declaration of absolution is. That which God alone can give always comes to us through the mediation of some part of the created order. So the experience of divine forgiveness does not offer the same kind of grounds for specifying the status of the one through whom that forgiveness has been mediated as does the declaration of sacramental absolution. The Pharisees in the story of Mark 2 and Athanasius in his polemic against Arianism put too much confidence in the inferential logic of their arguments.

So we need to be more prepared to acknowledge the problematic character of any move beyond the work of Christ that seeks to speak more directly of his person. Jesus is undoubtedly at the heart of what I have called the Christ-event. But what it is open to us to speak of is, at most, the transformative effect on those who have borne and those who continue to bear the imprint of his impact on their lives. There is nothing really very surprising in that, however. We are, after all, only persons by virtue of our interrelations with other persons, and we have already seen that many person statements do, in fact, focus on the role of that person as apprehended in the public sphere. But it does mean that in so far as our affirmations continue to take the form of statements about the person of Christ in relation to God, we must never lose sight of their irremediably complex charater. The 'person' of whom we will be speaking cannot be the person of Jesus *simpliciter*. It will be a composite reality, involving at one and the same time Jesus of Nazareth as he lived, the pictures of Jesus presented in scripture where his significance for his followers is variously discerned and partly created, and also the differing apprehensions of Jesus that have been affirmed and proclaimed in the subsequent life of the church.

It may be that the person and work of Christ stand to one another in the relation that Lee Keck's epigram so succinctly expresses, within the order of being. But if so, it is a relation of which we cannot speak without distortion of the evidence at our disposal. If the one is a necessity for the validation of the other, it is a validation we are unable to provide. We do better to see them as standing in a less linear, and more symbiotic, relationship as two aspects of a complex whole. The necessity that they impose on us is not so much a matter of tracing their relation to one another, as of placing them as a complex unity within a broader theology that seeks to make sense of God's dealings with the world as a whole. Christology will be likely to take on a somewhat different shape from the one which has dominated Christian history and which is still generally assumed to be appropriate today. What that new shape may turn out to be belongs to another occasion. But we need first to lay to rest the ghosts that so easily entice us to assay the wrong kind of enterprise, one that is doomed to failure at the outset because we do not have the kind of evidence that it would require.

13

The Meaning of Christ

This essay is being written as a tribute to John. John is a common name. If the context did not show immediately which John is intended, I would have needed to have given some additional indication. That would be done most simply by a further naming, by saying that it is for John Hick. But the same task could be achieved with the aid of a title of some distinguishing achievement of his. I could say it is for the Danforth Professor of the Philosophy of Religion at Claremont Graduate School or for the outstanding pioneer of a pluralist approach to religion among Christian theologians from the United Kingdom.

The essay is about Jesus. Jesus too was a common name. Again, if the context did not answer the question, which Jesus is intended, even more decisively, some further indication would have been called for. While we might say it is about Jesus-bar-Joseph, we would be more likely in this instance to make the needed clarification by way of a title or allusion to his distinguishing achievement. We might say it is about Jesus, the prophet from Nazareth, or about Jesus, the focal figure of Christianity. A vast number of titles have been given to Jesus. Origen lists over thirty of them, distinguishing between those like Wisdom and Truth, which indicate his fundamental nature, and those, like Good Shepherd or Lamb of God, which relate to more specific functions for the good of humankind.[1] Origen describes them at the outset as 'titles of Jesus', but more often in the course of his discussion refers to them as titles given to Christ. Yet Christ, the anointed one, figures also within the list of titles. Indeed, Origen not only puts it in his secondary, less fundamental category, but also argues that it is one that relates specifically to the human aspect of Jesus, since to be anointed implies entry into the office of king or high-priest, a process of becoming which in Origen's eyes is inapplicable to the unchanging eternal character of Jesus' divine nature. Thinking in more historical terms, we might be more inclined to represent it as embodying the affirmation that Jesus is the fulfilment of God's promises and purposes in relation to the people of Israel. But however we define its particular significance as a title, it stands out from all the other titles in that it alone came, quite early, to function not only as a title but also as a name, as we have already seen it doing in Origen's case. Although the particular messianic significance of the term 'Christ' has not simply been forgotten or fallen wholly into abeyance, 'Jesus Christ' can be used as a name without any intended reference to it. This transition from title to name is a well-known phenomenon. In the days of smaller, more static communities 'Johns' were distinguished as 'John the smith' or 'John the baker'; today we have simply our 'John Smiths' and our 'John Bakers'. They now function purely as names; both may turn out to be politicians or bishops rather than shoers of horses or makers of bread. 'Christ' is peculiar in that it has continued over a long period of time to function in both capacities, as a name and also as a title indicating a particular role. This ambivalence of connotation is not to be regarded as necessarily a negative factor. The play between differing senses over the range of possible meanings that can be given to a single term is a fundamental and creative usage in the writing of poetry; but it can cause misunderstanding in the development of a logical argument. Christian discourse incorporates both the poetry of immediate religious utterance and the prose of theological reasoning. In the latter case it is important to keep an eye open to see if variable uses of the word 'Christ' have given rise to confusion. One context in which the ambivalence of meaning attaching to the term 'Christ' has been much exploited, partly consciously, partly unconsciously, is the discussion of a Christian interpretation of other religions. My aim in this chapter is to look at the usage and to ask whether it is, in this case, a source of creativity or of confusion.

As a kind of prologue to the main issue I propose to discuss, it is worth recalling briefly the appeal to Christ characteristic of neo-orthodox rejection of any divine revelation outside the Christian sphere. For Hendrik Kraemer, Jesus Christ was the revelation of

God and the one authority in whose light every religion, including Christianity, was to be judged. Kraemer recognizes that people might be in some doubt as to how he intends 'Jesus Christ' to be understood in the context of that claim. To remove any doubt he states explicitly:

> By Jesus Christ I mean that Jesus whom we know from the total witness of apostles and evangelists in the New Testament: the Jesus who says . . . 'I am the Truth.'[2]

The problem of reference in this case is whether there is a single Jesus who says 'I am the Truth' to whom the New Testament as a whole bears a united witness. But even if that problem can be overcome there is a further question whether that Jesus Christ can be known in such independence of Christianity that he can serve equally as a judge of all religions, including Christianity itself. Kraemer has rightly indicated the need for a principle of criticism within Christianity, as well as within all other religions. But in identifying that principle with the Jesus Christ witnessed to in Christianity's canonical scriptures, he has not succeeded in avoiding the problematic claim of Christianity's assumed superiority over all other religions.

But the more enigmatic problem, towards which this chapter is directed, concerns the use of the term 'Christ' by many of those who do want to affirm a revelation of God in and through non-Christian religions but who do not want to espouse as full-blooded a religious pluralism as John Hick advocates. Other religions are uninhibitedly acclaimed to be the medium of divine revelation or salvation, but that revelation and that salvation are said to be the work of Christ. Thus D'Costa notes that

> Rahner does not concede a true pluralism in that he always affirms that all salvation is salvation, implicitly or explicitly, through the grace of God in Christ.[3]

Many other examples could be given from a wide variety of writers, using essentially the same language. Two examples will suffice. John Taylor declares:

We do not have to deny the reality of grace and salvation that are found, because of Christ, in all the faiths of mankind.[4]

And Julius Lipner expresses his conviction that we can say of 'most non-Christian religions of the world' that 'God through Christ operates from within their traditions and draws all men to himself'.[5]

What is the intended significance of the words 'in Christ', 'because of Christ', and 'through Christ' in the context of these affirmations? What is the relation of the use of the term 'Christ' here to its use as a name for Jesus of Nazareth? One answer, given by Raimundo Panikkar, is to see this way of speaking as deriving from the fundamental dogmatic principle that 'whatever God does *ad extra* happens through Christ'.[6] Those words come from the final paragraph of the Epilogue to Panikkar's book, *The Unknown Christ of Hinduism*, and he rather surprisingly describes them as 'a theological conclusion which is directly consequent upon [the] christological approach' he has followed. To me they appear more like a theological premise on which the christological approach is directly consequent rather than the other way round. But his way of putting it is perhaps a not-too-surprising feature of his discursive and imaginative rather than sequentially ordered style of reasoning. If it were simply a matter of faithfulness to the old dogmatic principle, which Panikkar's wording alludes to, it would be more natural to speak in terms of a work of the Father through the Son. Some further explanation is needed for the use of the term 'Christ' instead. Moreover, one might then expect the words to reappear in every statement about God's activity in the world, rather like some people's use of 'D V' in any statement of future plans. Something more needs to be said about the specific preference for the term 'Christ' in this context and the particular emphasis given to this universal principle of God's activity being through the Son or through Christ in relation to revelation in non-Christian religions. Panikkar's answer is to emphasize not merely the *ambi*valence of 'Christ', to which I have already referred and which he also acknowledges,[7] but the *poly*valence of its use as a symbol.[8] With ample grounding in New Testament usage, it has taken on a rich range of meaning in the course of Christian history, where 'Christ' has come to serve 'as that symbol which "recapitulates" in itself the Real in its totality'.[9] 'Christ' is, therefore, for Panikkar the natural and appropriate term to use in speaking of the cosmic or world-wide nature of God's activity.

Another form of basically the same answer relates specifically to the issue of salvation through the medium of other religions. In this case Panikkar does express himself in the deductive form that more accurately represents the structure of his argument.

> Christ is the universal redeemer. There is no redemption apart from him. Where there is no redemption there is no salvation. *Therefore*, any person who is saved – and we know by reason and by faith that God provides everybody with the necessary means of salvation – is saved by Christ the only redeemer.[10]

Here the logic of the argument is explicit. We know that Christ is the only and universal saviour. Salvation is to be found in and through non-Christian religions. Therefore Christ must be at work there and the salvation received there be salvation through Christ. But the clear logical structure of the argument requires us to ask questions about the consistency of the way the term 'Christ' is used. We have noted the ambivalence, or indeed polyvalence of its use. Is that ambivalence involved here in a way that might undermine the force of the argument? Is there an intended reference to the crucified Jesus of Nazareth in the major premise? And if so, is there an intended reference to him of the same order in the conclusion of the syllogism?

It is not easy to be clear about Panikkar's position on that question. It would seem that while he does not want to deny the link, he has chosen increasingly, as time has gone on, to play it down. In a further reference to redemption, a little after the one I have just quoted, he wrote in 1964: 'The Christian way is always one of co-redemption and there is no other redemption but in the cross.' In the revised edition of 1981, however, the last ten words with their reference to the cross are omitted.[11] Paul Knitter has drawn attention to a general move of this kind in Panikkar's thought over the period between the two editions in a helpful discussion, based on a much wider range of Panikkar's writings than has been available to me.[12] But on this crucial issue, Knitter appears to have overstated his case. In 1964 Panikkar wrote:

> The stumbling-block appears when Christianity further identifies, with the necessary qualification, Christ with Jesus, the Son of Mary. A full Christian faith is required to accept this identity.

Knitter cites this concern with the 'identity' of Christ with Jesus, Son of Mary, as something that Panikkar has moved away from since the 1970s. But the words are still there in the revised edition of 1981. Indeed the 'identity' is spoken of in the later revision as not merely required by a 'full Christian faith' but, if anything, more basically as that which 'characterizes the Christian belief'.[13] Panikkar's sense of what constitutes Christianity's self-identity does not allow him, it would seem, to abandon an identity between the Christ at work in Hinduism and the historical figure of Jesus, but his positive attitude to the underlying, and less historical, conceptions of Hinduism makes him keen to maintain at the same time a clear separation between them. The ambivalence of the term 'Christ' serves his purpose. But if the way it does so can be claimed to contribute to creativity, it seems liable to contribute to confusion also.

Panikkar is exceptional in the degree to which he seeks to loosen the ties between Jesus and the Christ who is the medium of God's revelation and salvation in other religions. The three writers whom I quoted earlier as representative examples of an insistence that God's revealing and saving work in non-Christian religions is 'through Christ' – Karl Rahner, John Taylor, and Julius Lipner – all want to insist on closer links than Panikkar implies. For the Catholic Rahner and the Evangelical Anglican Taylor the heart of the argument is the same. However universal the working of God's grace may be, it can only be so on the basis of its having one perfect and complete instantiation in the contingency of the historical order. D'Costa explains Rahner's use of the controversial term 'anonymous Christian' (rather than, for example, anonymous theist) as a description of anyone who responds to the grace of God, wherever and however it comes to him, as justified by the fact that 'all grace is teleologically directed to its explicit expression of the definitive self-revelation of God in *Christ*'.[14] And Rahner himself describes the Incarnation as 'the end and the goal of this world's reality', 'the point of climax in the development of the world towards which the whole world is directed' and 'a condition for the universal bestowal of grace to spiritual creatures'.[15] John Taylor makes essentially the same point in terms of his different theological background:

> What God did through Jesus Christ is the one act which it was always necessary that he should accomplish in time and at the right time if he were to be the God who throughout time is accessible and present to every human being in judgment and mercy, grace and truth.[16]

Once again there is a dogmatic principle at work in both writers, but one to which the role of the one, definitive and unrepeatable, historical act of God in the incarnation and crucifixion of Jesus Christ is integral in a way that it is not for Panikkar. How this dogmatic principle, with its talk of the necessity of a once-for-all divine action in Christ, can be known to be true, in advance of a deeper dialogue with those other religions in which the grace of God is also acknowledged to be operative, is beyond the scope of this essay.[17] For our present purpose it is sufficient to notice that it is this principle, which lies behind and gives substance to the use of the words 'in Christ' or 'because of Christ' in relation to the grace of God operative in non-Christian religions. Both aspects of the ambivalence in the meaning of 'Christ' have a significant role to play. Its function as a name for Jesus is an intended part of its reference, because there is a necessary link between his historical life and every other occasion of divine grace at work.

Lipner is even more explicit in making the traditional Catholic doctrine that Christ and his church are 'the necessary channel of grace for all mankind' the determining factor in his position. The basic understanding of that traditional doctrine is not changed, he says, by the recognition of its operation in major non-Christian religions like Hinduism; it is only the implications of its scope and range that are affected. How then does he see the relation of the 'unknown Christ of Hinduism' (a phrase which he himself explicitly allows)[18] to the historical person of Jesus? In an earlier article he states that 'except where another sense is clear, I use "Jesus" and "Christ" throughout as they are commonly used, viz. as proper names referring to one and the same person'.[19] Although in that article he sees 'major non-Christian religions like Hinduism' as 'salvific structures within the confines of their own development', he does not describe that salvific work directly as a work of Christ. They 'display the workings amid personal encounter of a wise and loving Deity' and we are free to acknowledge 'the stirrings of his [Christ's] spirit in alien tradi- tions'.[20] So there the salvific activity present in and through other religions is ascribed in less specific terms to 'Deity' or 'Christ's spirit'. But when in the later article he ascribes it more specifically to 'Christ', it is natural to ask whether the term is still being used as a proper name for the person who is also named Jesus or whether this is a case 'where another sense is clear'. It appears that the naming role of the term 'Christ' is still intended, though its title role is designed to accentuate one aspect of the person named. Lipner makes use of 'a dichotomy between Jesus as a human, culture-bound figure and his transcendent and unrepeat- able relationship to the Father as the Logos'. It is, in fact, the old two-nature christology in its Alexandrian form to which he appeals, though it is its use by contemporary theologians rather than its historical pedigree to which he draws explicit attention. John Hick's acknowledgment of the Logos as active in other cultures and other religions is good as far as it goes, but is not enough. The affirmation, in Lipner's view, needs to be related not merely to the Logos, but also explicitly to 'the Logos (in so far as this name refers to the historical figure of Jesus)'.[21] Lipner speaks here in terms of Logos rather than of Christ, because Logos is the terminology used by Hick whose views he is seeking to criticize. To make this point, he has to speak rather oddly of 'Logos' as a name. One can see, therefore, why he prefers to speak himself (with Rahner and so many others) of the wider operation of grace as work done 'through Christ'. The ambivalance of name and title is more naturally conveyed by the term 'Christ'. It will more readily suggest both the historical figure of Jesus as such while at the same time pushing 'the human culture-bound' part of the dichotomy away from our attention.

One writer who has reflected more explicitly and at greater length on the meaning of 'Christ' in such discussions is John Cobb. He begins by distinguishing between words which 'designate particular things or persons' and those which 'stand for concepts'. But many words have a vast range of meanings which may unite entities and concepts. These words are said to name images, and 'Christ' is one of them.[22] 'Christ' can therefore be said to name the process of creative transformation and the hope to which that process leads.[23] But ' "Christ" names also, and more certainly, the singular figure of a Nazarene carpenter.'[24] For Cobb 'the identity of Jesus with Christ' is 'a matter of literal truth'.[25] It is so because the principle of creative transformation is not just a force from outside that influences Jesus from time to time; it is constitutive of his very selfhood. The fact that the identity is complete does not mean that it is exhaustive or exclusive. There is no question, as with Rahner and Taylor, of any logical necessity inherent in the operation of divine grace which requires that it should be true only of Jesus. The selfhood of others could have been constituted in the same way. It is only 'so far as we know' that Jesus is unique.[26] So the polyvalence of the image named by 'Christ' encourages a mutually illuminating interplay between what we know of Jesus and what we experience as creative transformation, whenever it occurs. And experience certainly suggests that it occurs in and through other religions than Christianity. Where it occurs, for example in Buddhism, Christians will naturally name it as Christ at work. But they will not expect Buddhists to name it that way.[27] Their own use of the name of Christ is a true and appropriate use. But it is not necessarily the only valid or final way in which such creative transformation may be named.

Of all the writers we have considered so far, John Cobb is the freest in attaching a broader range of meaning to the word 'Christ'. Neither Rahner nor Taylor would quarrel with his understanding of it as creative transformation and as hope. And they would applaud his affirmation of its literal identity with Jesus. But because that identity is not exhaustive, it allows for a more flexible understanding of the forms that creative transformation or hope may take. When the Christian sees such creative transformation at work in other religions, he or she naturally speaks of it in terms of Christ. But that is his or her way of interpreting something which members of other religions will name differently. Yet it is not just a matter of alternative names. The Christian's understanding of creative transformation, implicit in the use of the name 'Christ', may properly challenge the understanding of such transformation that is implicit in those other religions. But the Christian's is not a necessarily superior understanding that has in the end to be imposed upon the other. For since Jesus, though a perfect embodiment of Christ, is not a definitively unique embodiment, the understanding that grows out of the union of the two in Jesus is not automatically decisive for all spheres where Christ is understood to be at work.

In the discussion so far I have been trying to tease out what is implied by the widespread tendency to describe the work of divine revelation and salvation in other religions as work done 'through Christ'. In conclusion I want to draw out those implications more systematically and give them some kind of evaluation. In the first place it is clear that such language is primarily addressed to a Christian audience or readership. D'Costa defends Rahner's use of the terms 'anonymous Christian' and 'anonymous Christianity' against the charge that it is offensive to the non-Christian by claiming that 'the reflection is not meant to gain approval by the Hindu or the Buddhist but is addressed by the Christian to his, and the Church's, own self-understanding'.[28] And Panikkar gives as one of the reasons for his choice of 'Christ' in *The Unknown Christ of Hinduism* the fact that the book is 'intended principally though not solely for a Christian readership'.[29] Certainly the intended readership of a book is an important factor in determining an author's choice of words and images. So we might describe the use of the term 'Christ' in the context of the discussion of a Christian understanding of religions as an appropriate form of Christian rhetoric. It can serve as a way of reassuring a hesitant church and reluctant Christians that the acknowledgment of God's grace at work in other religions need not be seen as in opposition to the experience of revelation and salvation that has come to them within the Christian church. The ambivalence of the term 'Christ' can well serve that creative purpose.

But these writings, as Panikkar acknowledges, are not 'solely' for a Christian readership. And Rahner explicitly discusses the response of the Zen Buddhist, Nishitani, to his conception of 'anonymous Christians'.[30] The Christian authors can, of course, underline the fact that it is their way of speaking about the divine grace, and there is no expectation that adherents of other religions should do the same. If Christians 'find themselves obliged to call this mysteric aspect "Christ"', says Panikkar, that is a mark of their recognition of Hinduism as a genuine religion. But a Hindu may speak of Rāma, Krishṇa, Īśvara or Purusha.[31] And Rahner can acknowledge the appropriateness of his Zen Buddhist interlocutor describing him as an 'anonymous Zen Buddhist' and express himself honoured to be the recipient of such a title.[32]

But once we recognize that the language has a role to play not only in intra-Christian discourse but also in interreligious dialogue, the question inevitably arises whether the 'through Christ' language is the most helpful to employ. It is not the only term that Christians have traditionally employed to refer to God's activity outside the sphere of special revelation or of the church. And even if no term, when transplanted from the internal discourse of one religion to play a part in interreligious discourse, will be altogether free of hidden assumptions or misleading associations, some terms carry a lot more negative baggage from the past than others. The term 'Christ' (however useful as part of an intra-Christian rhetoric) seems to have two serious disadvantages in the interreligious context. First there is the linguistic link between Christ and Christianity. It is very difficult for interreligious dialogue to take place without either the reality, or at least the suspicion, of an assumed superiority of one party over the other. The history of the attitude and behaviour of Christianity as an institution to other religious bodies in the past provides ample ground for such suspicion. And despite Kraemer's attempt to drive a firm wedge between Christ and Christianity, the initial assertion by Christians that the grace of God acknowledged to be at work in the other religious traditions involved in the dialogue is 'through Christ', can hardly avoid being heard as subordinating that religion to the institutional phenomenon of Christianity. Thus while the choice of 'Christ' language in this context may be seen as fulfilling a constructive role in the context of an intra-Christian rhetoric, it has also to be seen as fulfilling a negative role in the context of interreligious dialogue. Secondly, the fact that Christ (alone among the many titles of Jesus) is also a name for the historical figure of Jesus, adds to its problematic character in this context. Panikkar goes so far as to issue a warning against presupposing 'the Christian concept of Christ' with its emphasis on the historical particularity of Jesus.[33] We have already seen from Lipner's discussion that, when using the term 'Christ' in this wider context, Christians themselves have to appeal to a dichotomy in its application to the historical figure of Jesus, if their claim is to make coherent sense. Yet just because 'Christ' functions also as a name for Jesus, it conceals that dichotomy in a way that other titles which also relate to Jesus, such as Logos, do not. That would seem to make them less misleading titles to use in this particular context of interreligious dialogue.

The most obvious alternatives to speaking of divine grace in non-Christian religions as 'through Christ' would be to ascribe it to the Logos, as suggested above, or to the Spirit, or simply to describe it without further specification as the work of God. In distinguishing between these alternatives, it is not, of course, a question of determining which is the true account. It is a question rather of which fits better with the ways in which those differing terms are normally understood with respect to the activity of God, and which carry the more helpful associations for readers or for participants in dialogue with their diverse backgrounds.

The various writers with whom I have been concerned in this chapter do reflect occasionally on the grounds for their preference for the use of the term 'Christ' over the other three suggestions that I have put forward. Lipner, as we have seen, accepts the validity of the use of the term 'Logos' but prefers the term 'Christ' precisely because of its more obvious naming of the historical Jesus and its continuation of the dogmatic principle which affirms Christ to be the universally necessary channel for divine grace. It goes hand in hand with a desire (which he shares with several other Catholic writers) to maintain the claim that there is no salvation outside the church, in a way which extends the meaning of 'church' beyond the institutional church while at the same time keeping the links between the two as close as is consistent with that extension of meaning. In both cases, in respect both of 'Christ' and of 'church', the extended range of meaning makes, as it seems to me, for lack of clarity and confusion in understanding. The ambivalance inherent in the term 'Christ' is being stretched to the point of incoherence.

Cobb's preference for Christ over Logos is based on very different but also unsatisfactory grounds. Although he recognizes that in Christian history Logos has served as a bridge between divine transcendence and divine immanence, he sees 'Logos' as suggesting primarily a transcendent possibility and 'Christ' as designating that Logos incarnate throughout nature and history.[34] It is questionable whether that distinction represents either the main historical tradition or the most natural contemporary understanding of the terms. Cobb gives less consideration to the possible use of the term 'Spirit'. His suggested distinction of meaning between the terms 'Christ' and 'Spirit' is the priority of the link with Jesus in the former and with the goal of the Kingdom and of Resurrection in the latter.[35] Yet his own substantial discussion of Kingdom and Resurrection is entirely in terms of Christ as hope without reference to the Spirit.[36] He does not seem himself to use the pattern of differentiation he proposes. Without a more consistent distinction in the usage of the two terms, his own vigorous espousal of the term 'Christ' cannot carry great weight in the deliberations of others about the most appropriate term to use.

Panikkar's discussion of the relative merits of the terms 'Christ' and 'Spirit' in relation to other religions evidences an indecision in his own mind. He expresses a preference for 'Christ' over 'God' or 'Spirit' on the ground that the latter are not such living symbols.[37] But Christ's 'necessary identity with Jesus' is not for him the positive recommendation that it is for Lipner. He sees it rather as an inhibition on fruitful dialogue and at that point goes on to set out the advantages inherent in the use of 'Spirit'.[38] But they are evidently not strong enough in his eyes to become the determining factor in his own usage.

It is Rahner, with his more comprehensive and precisely articulated theological scheme, who provides us with the fullest and firmest grounding for an emphasis on Christ as the medium of God's salvation in other religions. We have already referred to D'Costa's explanation of why 'anonymous Christian' is more appropriate than 'anonymous theist': the incarnation is the indispensable condition of all God's gracious dealing with the world.[39] Rahner himself, in an article entitled 'Jesus Christ in the non-Christian Religions', lays great stress on the Spirit as the medium of his presence there. But he lays still greater stress on the fact that it is the Spirit of Jesus Christ. The historical event of the incarnation is the goal of all the work of the Spirit in our human world, so that Rahner can even affirm that 'Jesus is the "cause" of the Spirit'.[40]

It is that unqualifiedly determinative link between the historical figure of Jesus and the whole gracious outreach of God to the world that lies behind and justifies Rahner's insistence on Christ as the medium of God's self-communication to the non-Christian world. With him the ambivalence of Christ as name and title makes precisely the bridge he desires between the historical particular and the divine universal which faith apprehends but which human conceptuality finds it so difficult to provide. But not all Christians can tie the two together in so absolute a manner. Even John Cobb, as we have seen, despite his affirmation of an identity of Christ with Jesus, does not see that identity as a necessarily unique phenomenon, decisive for the whole process of God's gracious self-giving. And John Hick has argued on many occasions against any suggestion that such a view is a necessary corollary of finding salvation through Jesus Christ.

Christian recognition of God's revelation and saving presence in other religious traditions is a development to be warmly welcomed. To describe that work as work 'through Christ' can serve as a reassurance to Christians that there is no ultimate conflict between that revelation and saving presence and those experienced within the Christian church. But it also has, as I have tried to show, some serious disadvantages. It is likely to prove a source of intellectual confusion and of added difficulty to the already difficult venture of interreligious dialogue. And there are other ways in which that reassurance can be effected. The essential point seems to me to be more simply and more clearly made in language proposed by Wilfred Smith, with which I will bring this chapter to a close:

> A Buddhist who is saved, or a Hindu or a Muslim or whoever, is saved, and is saved only, because God is the kind of God whom Jesus Christ has revealed him to be . . . Because God is what he is, because he is what Christ has shown him to be, *therefore* other men *do* live in his presence.[41]

Notes

Introduction

1. Wolfhart Pannenberg, *Systematic Theology Vol. 1*, T. & T. Clark 1991, p. 18. Pannenberg ascribes its initial use to Quenstedt in the seventeenth century, and its more general adoption to the early eighteenth century.
2. Rowan Williams, *Arius*, Darton, Longman and Todd 1987, esp. pp. 233–45.

1 The Uses of 'Holy Scripture'?

1. C. F. Evans, *Is 'Holy Scripture' Christian?*, SCM Press 1971.
2. Ibid., p. 36.
3. Ibid., pp. 29–30.
4. Basil Mitchell, *The Justification of Religious Belief*, Macmillan 1973, pp. 155–6.
5. See Diogenes Laertius, *Vitae Philosophorum*, VIII 21.
6. Ps. 137.9.
7. W. Jaeger, *Paideia*, Vol. III, Berlin 1947, p. 269; ET Blackwell 1945, pp. 194–5.
8. A. D. Nock, *Conversion*, OUP 1933, p. 241.
9. S. G. F. Brandon, 'The Holy Book, the Holy Tradition and the Holy Ikon' in F. F. Bruce and E. G. Rupp (eds), *Holy Book and Holy Tradition*, Manchester University Press 1968, p. 15.
10. G. Widengren, 'Holy Book and Holy Tradition in Islam' in op. cit., p. 219.
11. M. Iqbal, *The Reconstruction of Religious Thought in Islam*, Kashmiri Bazar, Lahore 1962, p. 181.
12. T. F. Torrance, *Theology in Reconstruction*, SCM Press 1965, pp. 21–2, 58, 87–8; *Theological Science*, OUP 1969, pp. 22–3. Torrance himself gives to the distinction a far more comprehensive epistemological significance than I have in mind here, or indeed am able to accept.
13. Augustine, *Confessions* XII. XXIV–XXV. 33–4.

14. H. I. Marrou, *Histoire de l'éducation dans l'antiquité*, 6th edition, Paris 1965, p. 246; ET, *A History of Education in Antiquity*, Sheed and Ward 1956, p. 162.
15. Ibid., p. 333 (ET p. 224).
16. See W. Jaeger, op. cit., Vol. II, p. 289 (ET p. 214). Jaeger compares its authority with that of the Bible and the church fathers in the Christian era.
17. P. Brown, *Augustine of Hippo*, Faber 1967, pp. 259–60.

2 Scriptural Authority and Theological Construction

1. See David H. Kelsey, *The Uses of Scripture in Recent Theology*, SCM Press 1976, p. 89.
2. See Christopher Evans, *Is 'Holy Scripture' Christian?*, SCM Press 1971, pp. 1–36. The phrase 'the curse of the canon' is appropriately part of the oral tradition of Evans' teaching, not committed to writing!
3. See, e.g., the judgment of Leonard Hodgson in relation to the unitarian controversies in Britain in the 17th and 18th centuries, that '*on the basis of argument which both sides held in common, the unitarians had the better case. They could counter their opponents' biblical exegesis with interpretations equally, if not more, convincing*' (Leonard Hodgson, *The Doctrine of the Trinity*, Nisbet 1943, p. 223; Hodgson's emphasis).
4. See Colin E. Gunton, *Enlightenment and Alienation: An Essay Towards a Trinitarian Theology*, Marshall, Morgan and Scott 1985, p. 111.
5. For this term, see Hans W. Frei, *The Eclipse of Biblical Narrative: A Study in Eighteenth and Nineteenth Century Hermeneutics*, Yale University Press 1974, pp. 11–12.
6. Ronald F. Thiemann, *Revelation and Theology: The Gospel as Narrated Promise*, University of Notre Dame Press 1985, p. 83.
7. Ibid., p. 85.
8. Charles M. Wood, *The Formation of Christian Understanding: An Essay in Theological Hermeneutics*, Westminster Press, Philadelphia 1981, p. 100.
9. George A. Lindbeck, *The Nature of Doctrine: Religion and Theology in a Postliberal Age*, Westminster Press, Philadelphia 1984, pp. 120–21 (citing Kelsey, *Uses of Scripture*, p. 48).
10. Wood, *Formation of Christian Understanding*, p. 70; Wood's emphasis.
11. Thiemann, *Revelation and Theology*, pp. 65–66 (citing Wood, *Formation of Christian Understanding*, p. 43).
12. For a different assessment of what was implied by earlier claims that

scripture was a God-given unity, see John Barton, *Oracles of God: Perceptions of Ancient Prophecy in Israel*, Darton, Longman and Todd 1986, pp. 149–50.

13. Thiemann, *Revelation and Theology*, p. 86.
14. Ibid.
15. See Leslie Houlden, 'Trying to Be a New Testament Theologian' in A. E. Harvey (ed), *Alternative Approaches to New Testament Study*, SPCK 1985, p. 139.
16. Nicholas Lash, 'Performing the Scriptures' in *Theology on the Way to Emmaus*, SCM Press 1986, p. 44. Despite the title of the article, the actual discussion is exclusively in terms of the New Testament.
17. See Wood, *Formation of Christian Understanding*, pp. 72, 89.
18. For the first approach, see the passages cited in n. 11 above; for the second, see Thiemann, *Revelation and Theology*, pp. 5, 75–78.
19. See Lindbeck, *Nature of Doctrine*, pp. 92–96, 104–8.
20. The subtitle of Lindbeck's book *The Nature of Doctrine* is *Religion and Theology in a Postliberal Age*.
21. See pp. 44–45 above. See also J. L. Houlden, *Connections: The Integration of Theology and Faith*, SCM Press 1986, pp. 35–37.
22. John Barton, 'The Place of the Bible in Moral Debate' *Theology*, 88 1985, p. 207; Barton's emphasis.
23. Cf. the title of an article by Krister Stendahl: 'The Bible as a Classic and the Bible as Holy Scripture', *Journal of Biblical Literature*, 103, 1984, pp. 3–10.
24. John Hick (ed), *The Myth of God Incarnate*, SCM Press 1977.
25. See James Barr, *The Bible in the Modern World*, SCM Press 1973, p. 25. The whole section (pp. 23–30) is a useful survey of the various uses of 'authority' in relation to the Bible.
26. See John Fenton, 'Controversy in the New Testament' in *Studia Biblica 1978*, 3 vols., ed. E. A. Livingstone, Journal for the Study of the Old Testament Supplement Series 11, JSOT Press 1979–80, Vol. 3, pp. 97–100, with its judgment that there are only 'three books of the New Testament in the production of which, as far as one can see, controversy between Christians played no part' (p. 106).
27. Stephen Sykes, *The Identity of Christianity: Theologians and the Essence of Christianity from Schleiermacher to Barth*, SPCK 1984, p. 285. For the New Testament, see ch. 1; for Sykes' use of W. B. Gallie's 'essentially contested concept', see pp. 251–56.
28. See Maurice Wiles, 'In What Context Does It Make Sense to Say "God Acts in History"?' in Philip E. Devenish and George L. Goodwin (eds), *Witness and Existence*, University of Chicago Press 1989; reprinted below, pp. 153–63.
29. See n. 19 above.

30. Cf. Wood's use of that phrase, discussed on pp. 35–36, above.
31. The themes adumbrated in this paragraph are more fully discussed in my essay 'The Uses of "Holy Scripture"' in Morna Hooker and Colin Hickling (eds), *What about the New Testament? Essays in Honour of Christopher Evans*, SCM Press 1975, pp. 155–64; reprinted above, pp. 21–30.
32. See Maurice F. Wiles, *God's Action in the World*, SCM Press 1986, pp. 43–44.
33. See Houlden, *Connections*, pp. 35–37.
34. See Barr, *The Bible in the Modern World*, p. 27.
35. See David Tracy, *The Analogical Imagination: Christian Theology and the Culture of Pluralism*, SCM Press 1981, chs 3–5.
36. See n. 27 above.

3 Newton and the Bible

1. See R. S. Westfall, *Never at Rest: A Biography of Isaac Newton*, CUP 1981, pp. 309–10. This fine book includes much valuable discussion of Newton's theology, to which I am greatly indebted.
2. See F. Wagner, 'Church History and Secular History as Reflected by Newton and his Time', *History and Theory*, 8, 1969, p. 108.
3. Whiston is justified in claiming that if Newton had published his views on Christian doctrine as openly as he himself had done, 'they must 30 or 40 years ago have expelled and persecuted the great Sir Isaac Newton also' (*Authentic Records*, ii, 1728, p. 1080).
4. Keynes MS 6, p. 1 (Chadwyck-Healey Reel 18, No. 85: H. McLachlan, *Sir Isaac Newton: Theological Manuscripts*, Liverpool 1950, p. 58).
5. J. E. McGuire and P. M. Rattansi, 'Newton and the "Pipes of Pan"', *Notes and Records of the Royal Society*, 21, 1966, p. 108.
6. F. E. Manuel, *Isaac Newton, Historian*, Cambridge, Mass. 1963, pp. 38f.
7. R. H. Popkin, Foreword to J. E. Force, *William Whiston Honest Newtonian*, CUP 1985, p. xiv.
8. *The Correspondence of Isaac Newton*, iii, ed. H. W. Turnbull, CUP 1961, p. 233.
9. *Works of Richard Bentley*, iii, ed. A. Dyce, London 1838, p. 49. For Newton's role in relation to Bentley's appointment as first Boyle lecturer, see H. Guerlac and M. C. Jacob, 'Bentley, Newton and Providence', *Journal of the History of Ideas*, 30, 1969, pp. 307–18.
10. See H. G. Alexander, *The Leibniz-Clarke Correspondence*, Manchester University Press 1956, pp. 166–69.
11. See A. Koyré and I. B. Cohen, 'Newton and the Leibniz-Clarke Corre-

spondence', *Archives internationales d'histoire des sciences*, 15, 1962, p. 67.

12. Alexander, *The Leibniz-Clarke Correspondence*, p. xxii.

13. Ibid., p. 53. See H. Guerlac, 'Theological Voluntarism and Biological Analogies in Newton's Physical Thought', *JHI* 44, 1983, esp. pp. 226–29, and W. H. Austin, 'Newton on Science and Religion', *JHI* 31, 1970, esp. pp. 535f.

14. See F. Manuel, *The Religion of Isaac Newton*, OUP 1974, ch. 2, 'God's Word and God's Works'. Whiston speaks explicitly of the Light of Nature and Revelation as 'these two divine volumes' (*Astronomical Principles of Religion, Natural and Reveal'd*, London 1717, p. 242).

15. On the relation between Newton and the Boyle Lectures, see M. Jacob, *The Newtonians and the English Revolution 1689–1720*, Harvester Press 1976, ch. 7.

16. Yahuda MS 1, 1, p. 18 (C–H 34, 241) (Manuel, *The Religion of Isaac Newton*, p. 123).

17. W. Whiston, *Memoirs*, London 1749, p. 38.

18. Yahuda MS 1, 1, p. 19 (C–H 34, 241) (Manuel, 124). Whiston records that Newton was asked by Bentley if he could demonstrate the truth of his interpretation of prophecy, but 'was so greatly offended at this, as invidiously alluding to his being a mathematician, which science was not concerned in this matter, that he would not see him as Dr Bentley told me himself for a twelvemonth afterward' (*Memoirs*, pp. 113f).

19. Yahuda MS 1, 1, pp. 7–8 (C–H 34, 241) (Manuel, 113–14).

20. R. S. Westfall, 'Isaac Newton's *Theologiae Gentilis Origines Philosophicae*' in W. Wagar (ed.), *The Secular Mind*, Holmes and Meier, New York 1982, p. 16.

21. Letter from Locke to his cousin Peter King (30 April 1703) in Lord King, *The Life of John Locke*, ii, London 1830, p. 39.

22. *Correspondence*, ii, ed. H. W. Turnbull, CUP 1960, p. 327. The words are Burnet's summary of Newton's argument in a letter to Burnet no longer extant.

23. Ibid., p. 331.

24. MS Xa 'On the Motion of Bodies in uniformly yielding media' in J. Herivel, *The Background to Newton's Principia*, OUP 1966, pp. 307, 312.

25. *Correspondence*, ii, p. 331. On this topic, see esp. I. B. Cohen, 'Isaac Newton's Principia, the Scriptures and the Divine Providence' in S. Morgenbesser, P. Suppes and M. White (eds), *Science and Method: Essays in Honor of Ernest Nagel*, St Martin's Press, New York 1969, pp. 523–48.

26. New College MS 361 (2), p. 134 (C–H 24, 201).

27. *Observations*, pp. 4–11; New College MS 361 (2), pp. 132–34;

Martin Bodmer Foundation MS, 'On the Church', Introduction (C–H 33, 240).

28. New Coll. MS 361 (2), p. 132.
29. *Observations*, pp. 11f.
30. New Coll. MS 361 (2), p. 133.
31. *Observations*, p. 14.
32. Martin Bodmer Foundation MS, loc. cit.
33. *Observations*, p. 25.
34. See Westfall, *Never at Rest*, pp. 348f.
35. See Jacob, *The Newtonians*, p. 255.
36. C. A. Domson, 'Nicholas Fatio de Duillier and the Prophets of London', unpublished doctoral diss., Yale University 1972, pp. 50–55.
37. *Correspondence*, iii, p. 242.
38. Ibid., p. 245.
39. Yahuda MS 1, 1, p. 14 (C–H 34, 241) (Manuel, 120).
40. Yahuda MS 8, 2, p. 7 (C–H 37, 248).
41. *Observations*, pp. 238f.
42. See R. H. Popkin, 'Newton as a Bible Scholar' in J. E. Force and R. H. Popkin (eds), *Essays on the Context, Nature and Influence of Isaac Newton's Theology*, Dordrecht 1990, p. 109, n. 66.
43. See Westfall, *Never at Rest*, pp. 327f.
44. W. Whiston, *Six Dissertations*, London 1734, pp. 270f.
45. Keynes MS 5, p. 1 (C–H 18, 84) (McLachlan, 119).
46. Yahuda MS 1, 1, p. 15 (C–H 34, 241) (Manuel, 121).
47. Yahuda MS 1, 4, p. 28 (C–H 34, 241).
48. Yahuda MS 9, pp. 158f. (C–H 37, 249).
49. MS cit, p. 170.
50. *Observations*, p. 251.
51. Whiston, *Six Dissertations*, p. 329.
52. Ibid., p. 330.
53. *Observations*, p. 122.
54. See A. Tindal Hart, *William Lloyd 1627–1717*, London 1952, p. 177.
55. Yahuda MS 23, esp. p. 6 (C–H 40, 263). Whiston, who stood much closer to Lloyd than to Newton on this issue, describes such a view as 'a conjecture of Sir Isaac Newton's and I think a conjecture not well grounded neither' (*Historical Memoirs of the Life of Dr Samuel Clarke*, 2nd edn, London 1730, p. 96).
56. J. Barr, *Biblical Chronology: Legend or Science?*, University of London 1987, pp. 10f.
57. *Chronology*, p. 190. In an unpublished version (Yahuda MS 26, p. 38: C–H 41, 266) the word 'much' is omitted.
58. New Coll. MS 361(3), p. 166 (C–H 25, 202).

59. An amusing example of such detail occurs in Newton's correspondence where an unidentified writer is conveying to Bishop Lloyd Newton's praise for his 'many excellent observations . . . about the ancient year', but passes on Newton's reminder that, though the calendar month was normally corrected monthly by the new moons, 'Moses in describing the flood uses the calendar month not corrected by the course of the moon the cloudy rainy weather not suffering her then to appear to Noah' (*Correspondence*, vi, ed. A. R. Hall and Laura Trilling, CUP 1976, p. 34).

60. New Coll. MS 361 (3), p. 136 (C–H 25, 202).

61. *Chronology*, p. 358 (my italics).

62. Ibid.

63. McGuire and Rattansi, 'Newton and the "Pipes of Pan" ', p. 138.

64. Martin Bodmer Foundation MS, p. 138.

65. Keynes MS 7, 'A short scheme of religion', pp. 1–2 (C–H 18, 85) (McLachlan, pp. 48–51).

66. Yahuda MS 16, 2, p. 45 (C–H 39, 256). See Westfall, *Never at Rest*, p. 356.

67. Keynes MS 7, p. 3 (C–H 18, 85) (McLachlan, 52).

68. Martin Bodmer Foundation MS, ch. 1, p. 1 (C–H 33, 240).

69. See Westfall, *Never at Rest*, pp. 812–15.

70. *Correspondence*, iii, pp. 83–122.

71. Ibid., pp. 129–42. In almost all the 28 texts Newton cites, his judgment agrees with that of modern critical editions. But in some cases the 'corruption' he complains about is, as he acknowledges, something he has come across in only a single manuscript. Moreover, in many cases it is unlikely that there is any deliberate anti-Arian intention behind the variant readings he cites.

5 Person or Personification?

1. Published in N. Pittenger (ed.), *Christ for Us Today*, Papers from the Fiftieth Annual Conference of the Modern Churchmen, Somerville College, Oxford, 24–8 July 1967, SCM Press 1968, pp. 66–80 esp. pp. 79–80.

2. Ibid., p. 76.

3. I have in fact done so in discussion with James Dunn in *Theology* 85, March 1982, pp. 92–6 and September 1982, pp. 324–32.

4. Eusebius, *Contra Marcellum et De Ecclesiastica Theologia* (GCS, Leipzig, 1906), *Con. Marc.* 1. 1. (p. 7 ll. 3–7 and ll. 34–5). The scriptural evidence adduced by Eusebius is Gal. 4.4 and John 1.14.

5. J. N. D. Kelly, *Early Christian Doctrines*, A. & C. Black 1958, p. 240. Cf. J. T. Lienhard, 'Marcellus of Ancyra in Modern Research', *TS*, 43,

1982, p. 489: 'For Marcellus, the title "Son" applies only to the incarnate Word'.

6. Frag. 48 (p. 193); (p. 204).

7. In Frag. 42 (p. 193) the contrast is with 'Jesus or Christ'; in Frag. 43 (ibid.) it is with 'life, way, day, resurrection, door, bread'.

8. T. E. Pollard, *Johannine Christology and the Early Church*, CUP 1970, p. 253 (italics added).

9. Eugenius of Ancyra, *Expositio Fidei ad Athanasium*, 1, 2 and 4, 3. (See text of M. Tetz in *ZNW*, 64, 1973, pp. 79, 83.)

10. A. Grillmeier, *Christ in Christian Tradition*, 2nd edn Mowbrays 1975, pp. 279–81.

11. Frag. 129 (p. 215 ll. 4–5).

12. e.g. Frag. 52 (p. 194 l. 11); 60 (p. 196 ll. 3, 11–12); 61 (p. 96 l. 13).

13. Frag. 20 (p.188 l. 19). F. Loofs (*Paulus von Samosata*, Leipzig 1924, p. 239), who cites this passage as evidence for Marcellus's use of 'Son' as a title with reference to pre-existence, appeals also to Fragments 3 and 64, but both of these are capable of other interpretations.

14. The term 'pre-existence of Christ' is the normal form of words used in contemporary theology. I shall therefore use it here rather than the more cumbersome 'pre-existence of the only-begotten-Logos-Son', despite the fact that Marcellus would have strongly objected to our modern form of words.

15. *Ec.T.* 1.18 (pp. 78–80).

16. *Ec.T.* 1.1 (p. 63 ll. 4–8); *Ec.T.* 2.10 (pp. 110–12).

17. *Ec.T.* 2.10 (p. 110 ll. 24–6).

18. Ibid. (p. 110 ll. 26–30).

19. *Ec.T.* 2.9 (p. 110 ll. 15–22).

20. *Ec.T.* 2.10–11 (p. 112 ll. 6–17).

21. *Con. Marc.* 1.4 (p. 18 ll. 33–5); *Ec.T.* 1.17 (p. 77 ll. 9, 17); 1.18 (p. 80 ll. 7–10); 2.9 (p. 109 ll. 10–11; p. 112 l. 14).

22. *Ec.T* 2.17 (p. 121 ll. 10–11).

23. Frag. 58 (p. 195 ll. 15–17); 61 (p. 196 ll. 19–20); 62 (p. 196 ll. 25–6).

24. *Ec.T.* 2.13–14 (p. 114 ll. 10–35).

25. *Ec.T.* 2. 15 (p. 118 ll. 21–9).

26. e.g. *Ec.T.* 1. 1 (p. 63 ll. 8–9).

27. *Ec.T.* 2. 24 (p. 135 ll. 17–20).

28. Frag. 36 (p. 190); 63 (pp. 196–7).

29. *Ec.T.* 2. 20 (p. 127 ll. 7–27).

30. *Ec.T.* 2. 21 (p. 130 ll. 3–17).

31. *Ec.T.* 2. 18 (pp. 121–3). Cf. *Con. Marc.* 2. 4 (p. 57 ll. 16–30).

32. *Ec.T.* 1. 20 (pp. 80–98). The main Pauline texts cited are I Cor. 8.6; I Cor. 10.4; Phil. 2.5–8; Gal. 3.19–20; Heb. 4.14; Heb. 1.3; Col. I. 15–17.

33. *Ec.T.* 2. 14 (p. 114 l. 35–p. 115 l. 2).
34. Ibid. (p. 115 ll. 4–19).
35. *Ec.T.* 1. 20 (p. 80 l. 31–p. 81 l. 3).
36. *Ec.T.* 2. 14 (p. 115 ll. 2–4).
37. p. 194.
38. Frag. 61 (p. 196 ll. 20–2); 71 (p. 198); 116 (p. 209 ll. 27–8); 117 (p. 210 ll. 15ff.).
39. Frag. 60 (p. 196 l. 5); 121 (p. 212 ll. 10–12).
40. Frag. 117 (p. 210 ll. 15ff.).
41. The distinction between these two understandings, only the second of which involves a change in the subject, is clearly made by Aristotle (*De Anima* 2.5: 417^{a,b}) with use of the terms δύναμις and ἐνέργεια. For this point I am indebted to the Revd Dennis Minns and the Revd Dr Paul Parvis of Blackfriars, Oxford. The same general point is emphasized by A. Grillmeier, op. cit. n. 10 above, pp. 282–3, citing both T. Zahn and M. Tetz.
42. *Ec.T.* 1. 20 (p. 81 ll. 13–21).
43. J. D. G. Dunn, *Christology in the Making*, SCM Press 1980, pp. 243f.

6 Eunomius: Hair-Splitting Dialectician or Defender of the Accessibility of Salvation?

I am grateful to Thomas Kopecek and Anthony Meredith for helpful comments on an earlier draft of this paper.

1. M. F. Wiles, *The Spiritual Gospel*, CUP 1960, p. 147.
2. H. Chadwick, 'Eucharist and Christology in the Nestorian Controversy', *JThS*, n.s. 2, 1951, pp. 152–3 and 157.
3. Paul C. Empie and T. Austin Murphy (eds), *Lutherans and Catholics in Dialogue I*, Minneapolis, n.d. The date of the meeting at which the document was agreed was 1965.
4. H. M. Gwatkin, *Studies of Arianism*, Cambridge 1882, p. 266.
5. See R. C. Gregg and D. E. Groh, *Early Arianism*, SCM Press 1981. See especially pp. 50–70 under the sub-heading 'Adoption as Salvation: "Common to us and to the Son"?'
6. See M. F. Wiles (in collaboration with R. C. Gregg), 'Asterius: A new Chapter in the History of Arianism?', in R. C. Gregg (ed.), *Arianism: Historical and Theological Reassessments*, Philadelphia 1985, pp. 111–51, esp. pp. 138–40. [Since the publication of that article and of this essay, Wolfram Kinzig, *In Search of Asterius*, Vandenhoeck and Ruprecht, Göttingen 1990, has raised serious doubts about the reliability of Richard's ascription of those Homilies on the Psalms to Asterius.]

7. A. Harnack, *History of Dogma*, vol. 4, p. 74.

8. J. N. D. Kelly, *Early Christian Doctrines*, A. & C. Black 1958, p. 249.

9. See L. R. Wickham, 'The Syntagmation of Aetius the Anomean', *JThS* n.s. 19, 1968, pp. 532–69, esp. pp. 534–5.

10. J. N. D. Kelly, *Early Christian Doctrines*, p. 249. I have kept Kelly's translation, but it should be noted that both 'being' and 'essence' correspond to an original *ousia*.

11. Socrates, *HE* iv. 7.

12. Epiphanius, *Panarion* 76, 4, 2.

13. Theodoret, *Haereticarum fabularum compendium* 4, 3.

14. Chrysostom, *De incomprehensibilitate* 11 (*SC* 28, p. 154, lines 158–9); ps.–Athanasius, *Dialogus de sancta trinitate* 1. 1.

15. R. E. Heine, *Perfection in the Virtuous Life*, Philadelphia Patristic Foundation 1975, p. 135.

16. See Gregory of Nyssa, *Contra Eunomium* 11 (ed. Jaeger, vol. 1, pp. 268–9); *Ad Ablabium* (ed. Jaeger, vol. 3, pp. 44–5).

17. Paul Tillich, *Systematic Theology*, vol. 1, Nisbet 1953; SCM Press 1978, pp. 264–5.

18. Ibid. vol. 2, Nisbet 1957; SCM Press 1978, pp. 10–11. Perhaps similar critical pressure may be one reason for the varied forms in which the Anomoean saying we are considering has come down to us.

19. Eunomius, *Apologia apologiae* (in Gregory of Nyssa, *Con. Eun.*, ed. Jaeger, vol. 1, pp. 315.31–316.4); *Apologia* 8.

20. Eunomius, *Apologia apologiae* (in Gregory of Nyssa, *Con. Eun.*, ed. Jaeger, vol. 1, pp. 46.21–47.15); *Apologia* 16.

21. Eunomius, *Apologia apologiae* (in Gregory of Nyssa, *Con. Eun.*, ed. Jaeger, vol. 1, p. 282.5–7).

22. Eunomius, *Apologia* 9 and 24.

23. R. Vaggione, 'Aspects of Faith in the Eunomian Controversy', unpublished D Phil dissertation, Oxford 1976, p. 278. I am much indebted to Dr Vaggione for my understanding of Eunomius, through his thesis and through subsequent studies. His recent book, *Eunomius: The Extant Works* (OUP 1987) is an invaluable aid to Eunomian studies.

24. Gregory of Nyssa, *Contra Eunomium* III, 1 (ed. Jaeger, vol. 2, p. 39.13–14); Basil, *Epistula* 234, 1.

25. Gregory of Nyssa, *Contra Eunomium* III, 9 (ed. Jaeger, vol. 2, p. 284.16–18).

26. See my 'Soteriological Arguments in the Fathers' in F. L. Cross (ed.), *StPatr*, 9, 1966, pp. 321–5.

27. Justin, *II Apologia* 6, 1–2.

28. Justin, *I Apol.* 61, 10–11.

29. Origen, *Exhortatio ad martyrium* 46.

30. Origen, *Com. Jn.* 11, 13, 95; *Comm. Matt.* 17.36.

31. Origen, *De oratione* 24.2. Koetschau, the *GCS* editor, emends the MS reading *ōn* to *ho ōn* in line with the Exodus text, but the emendation is unjustified. Cf. the use of *ōn* by Basil of Ancyra in Epiphanius, *Panarion* 73.12 (*GCS*, p. 285 1.20) and by Eunomius, in *Apologia* 17.

32. Gregory, *Contra Eunomium* III, 8 and 9 (ed. Jaeger, vol. 2 pp. 251.16–279.23).

33. Eunomius, *Apologia* 17. (Cf. n. 31 above).

34. Cf. Gregory of Nazianzus's affirmation that *ho ōn* is uniquely indicative of God's essence, because unlike other basic titles, such as *theos*, it is not derived from some aspect of the divine activity (Gregory of Nazianzus, *Orationes* 30, 18).

35. Eunomius, *Apologia* 7–8. The Greek phrase is *tēn tou einai ho estin homologian*.

36. Basil, *Adversus Eunomium* 1, pp. 14–15 (*PG* 29. 546AB).

37. Ibid. 1, 13 (*PG* 29. 542C–544A).

38. Gregory of Nyssa, *Contra Eunomium* III, 9 (ed. Jaeger, vol. 2, p. 279. 22–3).

39. See Vaggione, *Aspects of Faith*, pp. 116–20.

40. Ibid., pp. 270–80.

41. *Clementine Recognitions* III, 3, 5–8; III, 7, 3–9.

42. See n. 37, above.

43. M. Harl, 'Citations et Commentaires d'Exode 3:14 chez les Pères Grecs des quatre premiers siècles', in *Dieu et l'Etre* (Paris 1978), pp. 87–108.

44. T. A. Kopecek, 'Neo-Arian Religion', in R. C. Gregg (ed.), *Arianism: Historical and Theological Reassessments*, Philadelphia Patristic Foundation 1985, pp. 153–5.

45. *Apostolic Constitutions* VIII, 5, 1; 6, 8; 12, 6; 14, 3; 48, 3.

46. Ibid. VIII, 5, 1.

47. John 17.3 was a text of great importance to the Arian movement as a whole. And *monos alēthinos theos* stands alongside *ho ōn* in the *Apologia* of Eunomius as the other scriptural phrase illustrative of titles referring directly to God (cf. n. 33 above).

7 On Being a Theologian in Today's Church

1. SPCK 1976.

2. E. Schillebeeckx, *Jesus*, Collins 1979, p. 39.

3. K. Rahner, 'On the Theology of the Ecumenical Discussion' in *Theological Investigations*, Vol. 11, Darton, Longman and Todd 1974, p. 38.

4. John McManners, 'The Individual in the Church of England' in *Believing in the Church: A Report by the Doctrine Commission of the Church of England*, SPCK 1981, p. 230.

5. David Tracy, *The Analogical Imagination*, SCM Press 1981, p. 29.
6. H. Richard Niebuhr, *Christ and Culture*, Faber 1952, p. 243.
7. K. Rahner, *Foundations of Christian Faith*, Darton, Longman and Todd 1978, p. 380.

8 The Reasonableness of Christianity

1. A much earlier version of this paper was read to one of our joint seminars. Some of the deficiencies of that version have been eliminated as a result of criticisms by Basil Mitchell and some helpful written comments by Robert Gay.
2. Cf. Locke, *Reasonableness of Christianity*, preface and section 252.
3. Cf. S. Toulmin, *An Examination of the Place of Reason in Ethics*, CUP 1950, p. 216. The importance of this general point is well illustrated by some words of Clifford Longley in *The Times* (17 September 1984): 'In a theological world pushed to logical conclusions there may be only three sustainable positions: Biblical fundamentalism, strict adherence to the Roman Catholic magisterium, or Cupittism: which may be why most people prefer to be a little illogical.'
4. P. van Buren, *The Edges of Language*, Macmillan 1972, p. 133.
5. Ibid., p. 147.
6. Ibid., pp. 146, 140.
7. P. Holmer, *The Grammar of Faith*, Harper and Row, New York 1978, p. 192.
8. R. Swinburne, *Faith and Reason*, Clarendon Press 1981; A. Kenny, *Faith and Reason*, Columbia University Press, New York 1983.
9. R. Swinburne, *The Coherence of Theism*, Clarendon Press 1977, p. 7.
10. Ibid., p. 70.
11. A. Kenny, *The God of the Philosophers*, Clarendon Press 1979, p. 5.
12. *Oxford English Dictionary*, vol. 1, p. 228.
13. Op. cit., p. 121.
14. Op. cit., p. 272.
15. Ibid., p. 233.
16. *Theology* 87, September 1984, p. 374.
17. Op. cit., p. 272.
18. R. Swinburne, *Faith and Reason*, p. 183.
19. Ibid., p. 177.
20. Ibid., p. 193.
21. Ibid., p. 192.
22. A. Kenny, *Faith and Reason*, p. 69.
23. Ibid., p. 72.
24. Ibid., p. 25.
25. For a fuller discussion see my *Faith and the Mystery of God*, SCM Press

1982, ch. 2.

26. Keith Ward, *The Concept of God*, Blackwell 1974, p. 156.

27. Cf. W. B. Gaillie, *Philosophy and the Historical Understanding*, Chatto 1964, chs 8 and 9.

28. For an excellent account of an approach to theological reasoning along these lines, see the work of Frank Burch Brown, in his article 'Transfiguration: Poetic metaphor and Theological Reflection', *Journal of Religion* 62, 1982, pp. 39–56, and more fully in his book *Transfiguration*, University of North Carolina Press, Chapel Hill 1983.

9 Worship and Theology

A version of this essay was given as the Aquinas lecture for 1990 at Blackfriars in Oxford, an institution which exemplifies in its life the combination of worship and theology discussed here. I am grateful to Dr Janet Soskice for helpful comments on an earlier draft of the essay.

1. B. F. Westcott, *The Epistle to the Hebrews*, Macmillan 1889, p. 356.

2. P. R. Baelz, *The Forgotten Dream*, Mowbrays 1975.

3. Anthony Kenny, *The God of the Philosophers*, OUP 1979, esp. pp. 128–9.

4. See A. Flannery (ed.), *Vatican Council II: The Conciliar and Post Conciliar Documents*, Costello 1975, p. 558.

5. See my *The Spiritual Gospel*, CUP 1960, pp. 68–71.

6. For this and the following paragraph, see my 'Eunomius: Hair-splitting Dialectician or Defender of the Accessibility of Salvation?' in R. Williams (ed.), *The Making of Orthodoxy*, CUP 1989, reprinted above, pp. 83–97.

7. G. Lindbeck 'Ecumenical Theology' in D. Ford (ed.), *The Modern Theologians*, Blackwell 1989, Vol. II, p. 267.

8. Ibid., p. 266.

9. Cf. J. M. Soskice, *Metaphor and Religious Language*, OUP 1985, p. 150.

10. Cf. my *The Making of Christian Doctrine*, CUP 1967, ch. 4.

11. Frank Burch Brown, *Transfiguration*, University of North Carolina Press 1983, p. 171.

12. D. .W. Hardy and D. F. Ford, *Jubilate*, Darton, Longman and Todd 1984, pp. 112, 113.

13. Soskice, op. cit., p. 141.

14. Brown, op. cit., p. 175.

15. Ibid., p. 177.

16. Hardy and Ford, op. cit., p. 115.

10 Can Theology Still be About God?

I am grateful to David Brown and Arthur Peacocke for helpful comments on an earlier draft of this paper.

1. See Robert W. Jenson, 'Karl Barth' in D. F. Ford (ed.), *The Modern Theologians*, Blackwell 1989, p. 25.
2. Gordon D. Kaufman, 'God as Symbol' in *God the Problem*, Harvard University Press 1972, p. 107.
3. Paul Tillich, *Systematic Theology*, vol. 1, Nisbet 1953; SCM Press 1978, p. 228.
4. Karl Rahner, *Foundations of Christian Faith*, Darton, Longman and Todd 1978, p. 192.
5. Wolfhart Pannenberg, *What is Man?*, Fortress Press, Philadelphia 1970, ch. 1, esp. pp. 3, 8.
6. See Wolfhart Pannenberg, 'Eschatology and the Experience of Meaning' in *Basic Questions in Theology*, vol. 3, SCM Press 1972, pp. 192–210.
7. Schubert M. Ogden, *The Reality of God*, SCM Press 1967, esp. p. 43.
8. Ibid., p. 20.
9. Gordon D. Kaufman, 'Christian Theology and the Scientific Study of Religion' in *God the Problem*, p. 34.
10. See Kaufman, 'God as Symbol', pp. 97–100.
11. See Michael C. Banner, *The Justification of Science and the Rationality of Religious Belief*, Clarendon Press 1990, p. 35.

11 In What Contexts . . .

1. *Theology* 74, July 1981, p. 245.
2. Maurice Wiles, *God's Action in the World*, SCM Press 1986.
3. Schubert Ogden, *The Reality of God*, SCM Press 1967.
4. Ibid., pp. 164–65.
5. Ibid., pp. 167–68.
6. Ibid., p. 179.
7. Ibid., p. 187.
8. Ibid., p. 179.
9. Ibid., p. 180.
10. Ibid., p. 184.
11. See my *God's Action in the World*, esp. ch. 8.
12. See David R. Mason, 'Selfhood, Transcendence, and the Experience of God', *Modern Theology* 3, July 1987, pp. 293–314, and Thomas F. Tracy, 'Enacting History: Ogden and Kaufman on God's Mighty Acts', *Journal of Religion* 64, 1 January 1984, pp. 20–36.

13. Austin Farrer, *Faith and Speculation*, A. & C. Black 1967, pp. 61–67.
14. Schubert Ogden, *Faith and Freedom*, Abingdon, Nashville 1979, p. 33.
15. See my *God's Action in the World*, ch. 6.
16. Stephen Toulmin, *An Examination of the Place of Reason in Ethics*, CUP 1950, pp. 145–51. The book is one much drawn upon by Schubert Ogden, especially in *The Reality of God*.
17. Article XXI: 'General Councils . . . may err, and sometimes have erred, even in things pertaining unto God.'
18. See my *God's Action in the World*, ch. 8.

12 Can We Still Do Christology?

I am grateful to John Fenton, Leslie Houlden and Robert Morgan for comments on an earlier draft of this paper.

1. H. P. Liddon, *The Divinity of Our Lord and Saviour Jesus Christ*, Rivingtons 1867.
2. T. V. Morris, *The Logic of God Incarnate*, Cornell University Press 1986, esp. pp. 161f.
3. Paul Tillich, *Systematic Theology*, vol. 2, Nisbet 1957; SCM Press 1978, esp. pp. 174, 131.

13 The Meaning of Christ

1. Origen, *Commentary on John* 1, 22–42.
2. H. Kraemer, *Why Christianity of all Religions?*, Butterworth 1962, pp. 15–16.
3. G. D'Costa, 'Karl Rahner's Anonymous Christian – A Reappraisal', *Modern Theology* 1, 2 January 1985, p. 139.
4. John Taylor, 'The Theological Basis of Interfaith Dialogue' in J. Hick and B. Hebblethwaite (eds), *Christianity and Other Religions*, Collins 1980, p. 224.
5. J. J. Lipner, 'Does Copernicus Help? Reflections for a Christian Theology of Religions', *Religious Studies* 13, 2 June 1977, p. 258.
6. R. Panikkar, *The Unknown Christ of Hinduism*, Darton, Longman and Todd 1964, p. 138; revd edn 1981, p. 169. The revised edition of 1981 incorporates significant changes to the earlier edition some of which are discussed later in the essay. Where the two editions overlap, page references are given to the 1964 edition, with the 1981 page nos. given in brackets. The wording of the quotations is from the 1981 edition.
7. Ibid. (1981), pp. 26–7.

8. Ibid. (1981), pp. 37–8.

9. Ibid. (1981), p. 28.

10. Ibid., p. 33 (pp. 67–8) (italics added).

11. Ibid., p. 42 (p. 76). For a similar omission of an earlier reference to the cross, cf. p. 18 (1964) with p. 50 (1981).

12. P. Knitter, *No Other Name?*, SCM Press 1985, pp. 152–57.

13. R. Panikkar, op. cit., p. 24 (pp. 56–57). Knitter, op. cit., p. 155.

14. G. D'Costa, art. cit., p. 135 (italics original).

15. K. Rahner, *Foundations of Christian Faith*, Darton, Longman and Todd 1978, p. 199 (= 'Christology within an Evolutionary View', *Theological Investigations*, 5, Darton, Longman and Todd 1966, p. 180).

16. J. Taylor, art. cit., p. 223.

17. I have discussed this question more fully in my *Christian Theology and Interreligious Dialogue*, SCM Press 1992, with special reference to Karl Rahner in ch. 3.

18. J. J. Lipner, art. cit., p. 257.

19. J. J. Lipner, 'Christians and the Uniqueness of Christ', *Scottish Journal of Theology*, 28, 1975, pp. 359.

20. Ibid., p. 365.

21. J. J. Lipner, 'Does Copernicus Help?', pp. 256–8, 251.

22. J. B. Cobb, *Christ in a Pluralistic Age*, Westminster Press, Philadelphia 1975, pp. 64–5.

23. Op. cit., pp. 24–5. Cf. also pp. 43, 45, 57–9, 183, 186.

24. Op. cit., p. 97.

25. Op. cit., p. 142.

26. Ibid.

27. John B. Cobb, 'Response II' in Leonard Swidler, John B. Cobb, Paul F. Knitter and Monika K. Hellwig, *Death or Dialogue?*, SCM Press 1990, p. 118.

28. G. D'Costa, art. cit., p. 133.

29. R. Panikkar, op. cit. (1981), p. 27.

30. K. Rahner, 'The One Christ and the Universality of Salvation', *TI*, Vol. 16, p. 219.

31. R. Panikkar, op. cit. (1981), pp. 26–7.

32. K. Rahner, ibid.

33. R. Panikkar, op. cit., p. 133 (pp. 164–5).

34. J. Cobb, op. cit., pp. 72, 76–7.

35. Op. cit., pp. 261–2.

36. Op. cit., Part 3, pp. 177–258.

37. R. Panikkar, op. cit. (1981), p. 27.

38. Op. cit. (1981), pp. 57–8.

39. See n. 14 above.

40. K. Rahner, 'Jesus Christ in the non-Christian Religions' *TI*, Vol. 17, pp. 43–6.
41. W. C. Smith, 'The Christian in a Religiously Plural World', in J. Hick and B. Hebblethwaite (eds), op. cit., pp. 105–6 (italics original).

Index of Names